Bensham, Gateshead The roof of a house was torn off by the 90mph winds of Storm Malik, which left 80,000 homes in the UK without power. Global warming is expected to increase the risk of storms. Photo: Owen Humphreys/Alamy

Mayfield, Manchester People arrive at the Repercussion Festival at Depot Mayfield on September 18, 2021. The 10,000-capacity venue is located in a former railway station on the 10-hectare brownfield site. Landsec completed its acquisition of Mayfield developer U+I in December, giving it a 50 per cent stake in the £1.4bn mixed-use project. Photo: Andy Barton/Alamy

Edge Road, Liverpool Plans to transform the Littlewoods Building into a £70m film studio have gained momentum since Liverpool City Region Combined Authority set aside £8m for developer Capital & Centric to undertake starting works. Anchor tenants include Twickenham Film Studios and Liverpool John Moores University. The Art Deco building's west wing was gutted by an arson attack in 2017. Photo: Jon Super/Alamy

Tobacco Dock, London Attendees focus on a neighbourhood planning workshop at the Festival of Place on 12 October, 2021. This year's Festival of Place will happen on 6 July, 2022 at Boxpark Wembley. Photo: John Sturrock

Wembley Park, London A family plays with Shadow Wall, an interactive canvas created by Jason Bruges Studio for Wembley Park, London. The artwork was commissioned by developer Quintain for the Royal Route underpass to create a memorable experience. Photo: Chris Winter

Elephant and Castle, London All that's left of Elephant and Castle shopping centre, but its iconic pink elephant sculpture lives on, perched on the roof of temporary shopping centre Castle Square, built by developer Delancey to house some of the displaced traders. Photo: John Sturrock

Sighthill, Glasgow A new pedestrian and cycling bridge over the M8 motorway connects the £250m Sighthill Transformational Regeneration Area with Glasgow city centre. Photo: Kay Roxby/Alamy

Newham, London Mayor Sadiq Khan moved the home of the Greater London Authority from its egg-shaped headquarters of 20 years beside Tower Bridge to the converted conference centre previously known as The Crystal in the Royal Docks. Richard Baker/Alamy

Briggate, Leeds Described as a message of hope and solidarity in two tonnes of neon, Dear Leeds was commissioned by the LeedsBID for the second year running. Inspired by Kate Ryrie's poem and created by James Glancy Design, it's been hailed as a celebration of "everything we are and everything we've been through". Photo: Gary Calton/Alamy

Bristol, UK Sage Willoughby, Jake Skuse, Milo Ponsford and Rhian Graham celebrate outside Bristol Crown Court after being cleared of criminal damage for pulling down a statue of slave trader Edward Colston during a Black Lives Matter protest in June 2020. Artist Banksy designed a T-shirt to raise funds for their defence. Photo: Ben Birchall/Alamy

Napier Barracks, Folkestone The 130-year-old Napier Barracks in Kent, used to house people seeking asylum, has been described as in "appalling" condition. Residents sleep in 20-bed dormitories separated by curtains. Clearsprings Ready Homes, which runs the barracks, has seen its profits soar, having secured Home Office contracts worth £1bn and paid out £7m in dividend. Photo: Gareth Fuller/Alamy

Royal Courts of Justice, London Ecologist Emma Smart (right) lends her support to a demonstration outside the Royal Courts of Justice. Smart served four months in prison for taking part in an Insulate Britain protest that blocked junction 25 of the M25 motorway. She undertook a 26-day hunger strike during her incarceration and was released on 15 January, 2022. Photo: Vuk Valcic/Alamy

the developer housing

Councils should lead the retrofit revolution for social housing, p72

Standard hotel, London, p.77

Houses in Multiple Occupancy are proliferating as landlords turn family homes into overcrowded bedsits, p84

Festival of Place 2022 goes to Boxpark Wembley on 6 July. p.90

partner content

These 94 new-build homes at North Forth housing in Leith, Edinburgh are divided into ground floor single-storey flats with a two-storey duplex above. Every flat has its own front door and private garden. The project was completed in 2018 for the Port of Leith Housing Association and City of Edinburgh Council by Collective Architecture with planning by Malcolm Fraser Architects. Photo: Woolver/Alamy

Planet Mark Business Certification to be awarded to residential developer, Mount Anvil

Having already been the UK's first residential developer to achieve Planet Mark's Development Certification, London based developer Mount Anvil is now set to achieve Planet Mark's Business Certification

Mount Anvil's Royal Eden Docks team with Planet Mark as part of COP26 Carbon Neutral Bus Tour

If you're not familiar with Planet Mark, the certification body works with businesses across the world to encourage climate action and build an empowered community focused on making sure the planet is fit for future generations. And by working with Planet Mark to achieve its Business Certification, Mount Anvil will be measuring its carbon emissions, reporting them, and reducing all associated with its business operations. This will enable the business to take a significant step in lessening its impact on the planet and society and creating a benchmark within the industry for others to follow.

Discussing the latest commitment from Mount Anvil, Steve Malkin, Planet Mark's founder and CEO, commented: "We're inspired to see the dedication to continuous improvement that Mount Anvil has made in committing to measure, report and reduce the carbon emissions associated with its business operations. As a developer focused on central London, the opportunity for Mount Anvil to deliver a positive legacy and lead from the front in the industry is enormous. As the first residential developer to achieve our Development Certification, measuring and reducing the whole-life carbon emissions associated with its builds, to now measuring and reducing the emissions associated with the business's operations through our Business Certification shows significant commitment and leadership.

"Mount Anvil's culture and stakeholder engagement marries perfectly with Planet Mark's three-step process to certification and the genuine passion for sustainability, showcased from the board right through to all of its employees, will ensure Mount

Anvil continues to deliver a legacy of positive change for many years to come."

Mike Valmas, head of preconstruction, energy and sustainability for Mount Anvil, adds: "Having undertaken Planet Mark's Development Certification process last year, we saw the huge benefit in deep diving into our carbon footprint at a scheme level. Understanding our impact on the planet will play a huge role in how we lessen it, which is why we're eager to further our commitment to climate action by working with Planet Mark to achieve their Business Certification. We have a huge opportunity to pursue better, differently, with their help."

Mount Anvil's environmental commitments extend well beyond traditional design and construction measures. Its work with Planet Mark includes commitments to protect an area of endangered rainforest thanks to Cool Earth, a charity working alongside rainforest communities to halt deforestation. With the help of Planet Mark and the Eden Project, Mount Anvil will also be expanding its schools programme which focuses on connections between people and the living world, exploring how we can all work together to build a better future.

"Our collaboration with Planet Mark is a brilliant example of what we look for in

our partnerships," explains Marcus Bate, Mount Anvil's partnerships and communities director. "It's different, ambitious, environmentally responsible and socially beneficial for communities and residents across London. The process of achieving the Business Certification has already helped us meaningfully improve our operational performance. Our collective focus on sustainability is now greater than ever before, and we've significantly improved the clarity of all our key performance indicators."

Mount Anvil has worked in partnership in London for the last 30 years, and is on a mission to pursue better, differently. Earlier this year the developer instructed JLL as its 2030 sustainability strategy advisors and also struck up new partnerships with Royal Botanic Gardens, Kew, The London Wildlife Trust and cycling charity Sustrans to support its sustainability and social value initiatives.

Shindigger brewery block party on Little David Street on Capital & Centric's Kampus development in Manchester. The cobbled street has permanently reopened to the public after decades behind gates. Photo: Jack Kirwin

Supply and demand is not going to fix the housing crisis, that much is clear

Christine Murray on why homelessness in the UK, like child hunger, is a policy decision

At a time when faith in people and trust in politicians is a fragile, broken thing, a good friend asked whether there would be any hope in this issue of the magazine – cracks where the light gets in. We need hope, she said, to find purpose in those video calls and emails; to envision future places where people thrive; to cope and carry on doing our best work in a system that values profitability over people.

I didn't commission any hope. That's not what editors do. I asked journalists and photographers to seek out answers to gnawing questions about housing. What does the government actually mean when it sets a target of 300,000 homes? What kind of homes, and for whom? Why is home ownership in the UK falling despite politicians banging on about it? What's stopping the widespread use of MMC and prefabrication? Are we going to "insulate Britain"? What is the local experience of Nine Elms, beyond the swimming pool in the sky?

Hope snuck on to the pages anyway. I spotted it looking askew next to the facts. There was hope in Emma Warren's report on how Finland is eradicating homelessness. Hope also stole its way into Laura Mark's article on social housing designed by Peter Barber Architects, which celebrates the joy of the city street.

I found hope elsewhere too, in unlikely places – pockets of resistance, stories about inequality, policy failures. Hope glued itself to one of the pages in protest, started singing *A Change is Gonna Come*.

Then hope was lost. Where did it go? It faded because we know how to solve the housing crisis, and yet the rate of homelessness keeps rising due to a shortage of social housing and cuts to benefits. Homelessness in the UK, like child hunger, is a policy decision.

It died because sometimes a problem is not the absence of a solution but a lack of impetus. Although I'm glad hope was found in these pages, its presence is unwarranted so long as we have a government adherent to the fundamentalist belief that good politicians just do nothing and let the market decide.

As Kate Raworth taught us in *Doughnut Economics*, supply and demand has always

Christine Murray. Photo: Anthony Coleman

been a seductive economic fallacy, and this is especially true of housing, not least because land is a finite resource. The housing market is shaped not only by the actions of homebuyers and sellers but the forecasts of investors and speculators, the cost of land, the value of rent, the permissiveness of planners, availability of bricks, quality of schools, and the infrastructure. In his article for this edition, Steve Taylor explains why the property valuation holds more sway than people in need of a home.

Government, not business, needs to lead – they're called "leaders" for a reason. Chronic under-investment in infrastructure by the private water companies provides the most basic example of where the market fails us. Tens of thousands of housebuilding projects are on hold across the country due to nitrate pollution or water shortages, following notices from Natural England. There is no reason to believe that private water companies will invest in a collapsing sewage system. They have no reason to. There is, however, reason to believe that they'll continue to pay out dividends – £57 billion worth in the decade to 2019.

As for air pollution, no single private company is responsible and none stand to benefit from air improvement. Without government leadership – carrot and stick – there will be no progress. Which is why the failure to tackle water and air pollution in the Environment Act is a blow. Who is the government protecting?

The Environment Act was a downer, but it's hard to choose the most disappointing bill in a straight run of lemons: the Police, Crime, Sentencing and Courts Bill, the Judicial Review and Courts Bill, the Elections Bill and the Nationality and Borders Bill all contain curbs on human rights that disproportionately affect women, people seeking asylum and racialised ethnic groups – including the right to strip any dual citizen of their British citizenship, without appeal and without explanation.

The Conservative party claims to stand up for the economy, but it appears to be defending only a relatively small number of corporate interests. It's not good for business to have hungry workers struggling to make ends meet. If people are the engine of the economy, that engine is running on fumes.

The white papers, reports and inquiries come and go with frenetic regularity but little meaningful action is taken to improve the quality of life. As we go to press, there is talk on the radio of a cost-of-living crisis that will "only get worse" with food and fuel prices rising. House prices in January 2022 have seen their fastest growth in 17 years. Homelessness has been rising every year for the past five years – and many people are made homeless because they can't afford their rent. The average age of death for people without a home is 45 for men, and 43 for women.

The Levelling Up paper was a disappointment too – old promises and no new money, with part of the report lifted directly from Wikipedia.

We've walked these gaslit corridors before, through the miasma of global warming, always waiting for the next climate report, another bill, COP26. And yet despite the occasional bombast of declaration, the money and political leadership has never adequately materialised. And so it is with housing.

Other countries are leading the way: Finland is close to eradicating homelessness; and then there's Italy's superbonus energy-retrofit programme. The latter has created 153,000 jobs and boosted GDP by 0.7 per cent while delivering home improvements at speed and scale. It's expected to cost €33 billion by 2036. There have been cases of

The housing market is shaped not only by the actions of homebuyers and sellers, but the forecasts of investors and speculators, the cost of land, permissiveness of planners, availability of bricks, quality of schools and the infrastructure

Urban Splash is part-way through its reworking of Park Hill, Sheffield. When complete, it has been said that around a quarter of the homes will be social rent. Originally built between 1957 and 1961, Park Hill was home to 995 council flats. Photo: TeamJackson/iStock

fraud associated with the programme, with estimates of up to €1 billion lost – though this is still a fraction of what the UK government squandered on unusable PPE.

In our previous issue, New Normal in 2020, I tried to capture a slippery moment in time as we emerged from the first Covid lockdown, seeking to catch, like fireflies in a jar, ideas sparked by that sudden and strange shift in working and living.

There's been a longer than usual gap between that magazine and this one – 2021 was a challenging year for independent media and events. I want to take a moment to thank all of you who attended our festivals and supported our journalism. If you love what we do, please consider joining us as a member.

The shock of the pandemic may have passed, but we are still in transition. Even as politicians encourage a full return to the office, there's a collective acceptance that a cultural change has taken place – we're just not sure what that means yet. Will we settle on two days in the office or will it be a four-day working week? Like teenagers, we don't know what we want, we have a hard enough time deciding what to wear. For this industry, preoccupied with the specifics of floorplates and tenures, flexibility is key.

As for housing – the theme of this issue – it feels like that's all anyone ever talks about. But we fail to address the elephant in the room: affordability.

This year's annual gathering, The Festival of Place is happening at Boxpark Wembley on 6 July, 2022 Photo: Lionel Derimais/Alamy

> A change has taken place, we're just not sure what it means yet. Will we settle on two days in the office or will it be a four-day working week? Like teenagers, we don't know what we want, we have a hard enough time deciding what to wear

It makes economic sense to solve the housing affordability crisis – a recent report from the Levelling Up all-parliamentary group and the Northern Health Science Alliance shows a £30 billion loss in economic productivity due to poor health in deprived neighbourhoods – even if people in those neighbourhoods work more hours than the average citizen. Overcrowding, homelessness and non-decent homes are a health and productivity issue. We need more homes for social rent – retrofitted, built or bought for people who need them most, supplied in the right places in cost-effective ways. We've done this before and we can do it again.

It's irrational to hope for government action at this time. But I find hope in this growing community of developers, public servants, investors, designers and architects. The rise in ESG investment, community engagement, co-housing, the B-Corp, community land trusts, net-zero commitments, biodiversity net gain and social value targets speak to the emergence of a purpose-driven industry committed to making a positive impact.

As this community grows – and it is growing – it will get noisier. The property and construction industry holds sway as a lobby. We are here to amplify your messages. The Festival of Place is critical to this mission too, bringing us together to learn and workshop ideas. We'll be coming together four times this year: in-person at Boxpark Wembley on 6 July, and online with Festival of Place: Social Impact (1-3 March), The Pineapples (23-27 May) and in November, with Festival of Place: Climate Resilience. If I can squeeze in one more hope, it's to see you there.

Christine Murray is founding editor-in-chief of The Developer and director of the Festival of Place. She is previous editor-in-chief of The Architects' Journal and The Architectural Review, where she founded the Women in Architecture (now W) Awards

For more information about the Festival of Place visit www.festivalofplace.co.uk

Has the "housing crisis" become a permanent condition?

The government repeats its target to build 300,000 new homes a year, but never hits it. Steve Taylor digs into the failure to build homes and the impossible dream of a home-owning democracy

Residents watch Notting Hill Carnival from a west London council block. Photo. Janine Wiedel Photolibrary/Alamy

Housing in the UK is yet again in crisis – an observation that has been repeated with such frequency over the past 30 years that it now indicates a seemingly permanent state of affairs.

The phrase "housing crisis" first appears in British English publications at around the end of the Second World War, with a vertiginous spike in 1988, the year the Housing Act ended rent controls, making property a much easier and more attractive investment. In 2019, usage of the term was heading steeply towards a similar, if not higher, peak. Yet despite the familiar formulation, the housing crisis is far from a single phenomenon; it's a toxic brew of socio-economic issues that had been simmering for decades before the 2008 financial crash and has since reached boiling point.

Official government acknowledgement of this state of crisis is enshrined in its "aspiration" to build 300,000 new homes a year. But how helpful is a single number? Housing priorities are anything but singular.

The needs of the quarter of a million people in temporary accommodation, the half a million people "sofa-surfing" or the more than a million on the waiting list for social housing are somewhat different to the "need" felt by a cabinet minister with a £100 million property portfolio for another multimillion-pound townhouse.

The government puts forward a precise typology of housing tenures, including affordable rent, social rent, intermediate rent, affordable home ownership (shared ownership and help to buy). Yet when asked via a Freedom of Information request by *Inside Housing* in March 2021 for its breakdown of the 300,000 target by tenure, the response was that no such analysis had been carried out. Worse still, these tenure types are not supported by any agreed definition of "affordable housing" with the result that, according to the 2020 review by the Affordable Housing Commission, many of them "are clearly unaffordable to those on mid to lower incomes".

The drive behind the 300,000 target began at the 2015 Conservative Party conference when prime minister at the time David Cameron announced the beginning of a "national crusade to get houses built". It was quantified in 2017 by then-chancellor Philip Hammond, while Cameron's successor, Theresa May, said meeting the target was her "personal mission". The number has been repeated by Conservative politicians in every subsequent parliament. In contrast, the Labour Party, in its 2018 report *Housing for the Many*, made a commitment to "build one million new genuinely affordable homes over 10 years"; the Liberal Democrats appear

to have swallowed the 300,000 target whole, though with the proviso that a third would be for "social rent"; and the Green Party has pledged to build 100,000 new "council homes" each year.

With the Conservative Party using its majority to set both the political agenda and, increasingly, the very terms on which crucial social issues can be talked about and debated, the 300,000 target has serious political and ideological heft behind it.

But is it the right number? Attempting to answer that apparently basic question is akin to voluntarily melting your brain, such are the complexities that imbue this country's housing needs and the possible solutions to them. But before diving into the maelstrom, here's the spoiler: the 300,000 number is almost entirely political.

How so? Conservative governments have repeatedly dismissed clear evidence that the statistical basis used to calculate the figure is outdated and incorrect. Every time it has been demonstrated that the data used to calculate society-wide home-building requirements indicates a different – inevitably lower – target, ministers have bullishly reinstated the 300,000 number. In 2018, for example, the Office of National Statistics (ONS) took over responsibility for forecasting housing requirements from the Ministry of Housing, Communities and Local Government (MHCLG – now the Department for Levelling Up, Housing & Communities) and immediately downgraded projections by 24 per cent in response to data showing that household size had stabilised rather than continuing to shrink. The MHCLG proceeded to dismiss the new data, ordering councils to use its own out-of-date numbers for estimating local house-building targets. Defending its stance, it said: "Methodological changes are not a reason why the government should change its aspirations … of supporting a market that delivers 300,000 homes."

Dismissing the notion that those aspirations can be met by "supporting a market", critics of government policy such as Polly Neate, chief executive of housing charity Shelter, point out that the last time anywhere near 300,000 homes were built in a single year, councils built over 40 per cent of them. In spite of numerous critiques, many in the field accept the political target uncritically – a clear indication of how it has become embedded in received wisdom about housing.

Shifting attention to another related metric for a moment, you might think it easier to determine the number of new homes actually built. Not so. Take 2019. According to the ONS, 178,790 new homes were built in England that year, whereas

the BBC quotes the much higher figure of 247,000 – a number that, it turns out, quantifies what government statistics refer to as "net additional dwellings" or "net change in the dwelling stock", including "new house-building completions", "gains or losses through conversions", "changes of use", "demolitions" and "other changes to the dwelling stock (caravans, houseboats etc)". Despite these ways of increasing the stock of "dwellings", the department arrives at a "new house building completions" figure of 220,600. All these numbers deviate from another official government source, the quarterly "Live tables on housing supply: indicators of new supply", which record 178,300 permanent dwellings completed over the course of 2019. To complicate matters further, these figures are partly derived from different sources.

Given that most people have neither the time, patience nor expertise to fully unravel the numbers, 300,000 is an effective rallying cry because it speaks to a folk economics view of how housing works. It's of a piece with the misleading "household budget" metaphor for the workings of the British economy. A big number – any big number, really – sounds good if you believe that housing is a simple case of supply and demand with the solution a straightforward matter of matching one to the other. Many "experts", especially those sympathetic to Conservative housing orthodoxy, support and actively promote this view, as did Gerard Lyons, chief economic adviser to Boris Johnson when he was mayor of London. His report for the centre-right think tank Policy Exchange early in 2021 called for a house-building boom to provide affordable properties on a "massive scale".

Unfortunately, not only is it just as tricky to pin down real demand as it is actual supply, but the task is made doubly difficult because house-building is not one market but two: one for homes and another for investment. Sometimes the two are

Nearly half of the homes sold under Right to Buy end up in the hands of private landlords, many of whom let to tenants who receive housing benefit. The faux-democratic boosterism accompanying the scheme therefore belies a massive transfer of public money to the private sector.

A library in Prestatyn, Wales which will be replaced with council flats and commercial space. Photo: John David Photography/Alamy

A protestor calling for action on homes walks past an advertisement for private flats in Peckham, London. Photo: Peter Marshall/Alamy

The Grade-II* Alexandra Road estate, completed in 1978, was the first post-war council estate to be listed. Designed by Neave Brown at the Camden Council architects department, the estate is home to 520 apartments, a school, community centre, youth club and park. Lois GoBe/Alamy

embodied in the same physical property, as when parents buy a family home with the assumption that in the future they will be able to rely on an increase to its value to fund deposits for their young-adult children's own house purchases. These contradictions lead to what has been dubbed the *Daily Mail* dichotomy: the idea that you want house prices to be as high as possible if you own one, but as low as possible for your kids to get on the housing market.

Leaving aside, for the moment at least, the ethics of leaving the delivery of a fundamental human right to a market mechanism, the fact that there are two versions of housing operating simultaneously – sometimes within the same physical property – with fundamentally antithetical aims has enormous bearing on the crisis and its potential solutions.

You can only participate in the market for houses and flats as an investment if you can afford to buy one, a situation exacerbated by the British tendency to regard home ownership as a universal life-goal. Cross over into the other market, the one in which people are simply trying to secure a roof over their heads, and the option of buying is a reality for fewer and fewer people, particularly the "generation rent" of young adults. This is down to a range of factors including escalating prices, job precarity, student debt, low wages that make it impossible to save towards a deposit and the swallowing-up of generational equity in funding parents' old-age care.

If you can't afford to buy, you rent, and move from being a potential beneficiary of the market to one of its victims. Whereas mortgage payments typically take up less than 20 per cent of monthly earnings, rent, depending on where you live, can range from 20 per cent of income right up to a crippling 40 per cent in London. On average, renters spend double the proportion of their monthly income on housing than buyers do.

Looked at from the supply side, renting is predicated on businesses, institutions and individuals owning residential property, all of which share a common feature: someone other than you gets to bank the gains. It is important to benchmark the fact that the supply side of housing has been subject to a "revolution from above" for the past four decades, from the great era of postwar social housing to a period of escalating privatisation.

The pivot between these was, arguably, Margaret Thatcher's Right to Buy policy, which has seen just under two million homes transferred from public to private ownership. The scheme has been discontinued in Scotland and Wales and will end in Northern

Energy-efficient council houses on the Knight's Close development in Top Valley, Nottingham. Photo: Tracey Whitefoot/Alamy

Ireland in August 2022, leaving it operating solely in England. It continues to hamper councils' capacity to provide homes as it depletes housing stock and syphons public money out of the system by mandating that sales are made at a significant discount and imposing stringent rules of how much of the resultant cash can be spent by recipient councils on building or buying new homes.

Nearly half of the homes sold under Right to Buy end up in the hands of private landlords, many of whom let to tenants who receive housing benefit. The faux-democratic boosterism accompanying the scheme therefore belies a massive transfer of public money to the private sector. To replace the social homes lost would cost, at today's prices, a staggering £276 billion.

Since 1980, the privatisation juggernaut has steadily gathered pace through the tenure of both the Conservatives and Labour before accelerating sharply under the Johnson government with a number of radical developments that, while apparently designed to boost the supply of houses as homes, substantially benefit the market for houses as investments.

Recent legislation, for example, allows

for-profit enterprises to call themselves housing associations as long as they sign on as registered providers with the Regulator of Social Housing. For-profit housing associations have been able to take in large-scale investment, the most controversial example being Sage Housing, which sold 90 per cent of its equity to Blackstone in 2017, extending to the UK the American private equity behemoth's strategy of investing in huge swathes of affordable housing. Here, the target is Section 106 properties, social housing built by developers. Blackstone enables Sage in bulk-buying on a huge scale – 7,000 homes valued at more than £1 billion – raising fears that smaller affordable-housing suppliers may be left at a competitive disadvantage. Compared to traditional housing association financing, in which surpluses must be ploughed back into more house-building, the Sage/Blackstone model is extractive, with an 8 per cent minimum return expected from a "global base of long-term institutional [limited partnership] investors, whose money comes from pension and endowment funds".

Then there's the car-crash that was the government's "starter home" programme, launched in November 2015 with a purported £2.3 billion budget. The National Audit Office (NAO), reporting on the scheme in November 2019, found that MHCLG had spent £174 million acquiring sites for the construction of 5,998 houses. It said it was "possible" that developers had built homes that met the necessary criteria, but they could not have been sold under the starter banner because the enabling legislation had not been passed by parliament. The NAO also noted that in July 2018, at the end of his short tenure as housing minister, Dominic Raab had claimed that £250 million had been spent solely on land acquisition; the statement "clarified" that building had not yet started. The NAO's frustration at the impossibility of securing any reliable data on housebuilding from the government is palpable in the wording of the report.

Help to Buy, introduced in 2013, has been excoriated by both the National Audit Office and the Public Accounts Committee for, once again, failing to make any contribution to solving the dearth of new affordable homes. Instead, its critics say, it has inflated property prices and housebuilders' profits. Then there is Shared Ownership, a government scheme to help home buyers who struggle to raise an initial deposit. It allows them to purchase a 10-75% share of the property and pay rent on the remaining equity, which the owner – usually a housing association – retains. They can also increase the share, which is known as staircasing. Shared Ownership has enabled around 157,000 households with a combined income of £80,000 or less to buy homes. But there are frequent complaints from Shared Ownership 'owners' in the press who feel trapped by the scheme. Problems include the escalating cost of monthly service and maintenance charges, which are owed in addition to rent and mortgage payments, the fact that owners are often barred from subletting the properties, and unsellable homes due to negative equity – an acute problem due to the cladding and fire-safety scandal having written the value of many properties down to zero.

Shared Ownership has proved a juicy prospect for big institutional investors, however. As estate agent Savills observes: "These sources of income come with relatively little risk. The repossession rate for Shared Ownership properties was just 0.02 per cent, less than half the level for general owner occupation at 0.05 per cent." Even where the stated goal is to provide nominally affordable housing, profit-seeking entities are either already firmly entrenched or are poised to make a killing.

Where exactly does that leave the 300,000 target? Those rooting for the further financialisation of housing (ie actual and potential beneficiaries from the process) promote increasing housing supply as the best way to reach the government's goal. Even setting aside the questionable nature of that figure – and the serial annual failure to achieve it – we are still left with the critical issue of which homes are being built and are likely to be built by the private sector. A singular, monolithic target for housebuilding is supremely unhelpful; what matters is what kind of homes are being built, where they are located and who they are for.

Conventional market wisdom enshrines two foundational – and demonstrably false – beliefs: that building more houses will reduce prices; and that the private sector can be incentivised, legislated and persuaded into producing homes for lower-income households.

The first, the supply and demand fallacy, states that in a theoretically free market, increasing supply will cause prices to fall. But the housing market is anything but free, not least owing to something called the market absorption rate. When a developer has all its ducks in a row to start building homes – a site, land purchases, planning permission secured, finance in place and so on – it doesn't just crack on with constructing and making available the total promised housing stock. If the timing is not right, that could reduce prices – useful for people wanting to buy a home but potentially ruinous for the housebuilder because of the valuation. The price of the land purchased is based on projections of what the homes will sell for. It is essential that the sale prices are maintained or the whole development will lose money. Oliver Letwin's independent 2018 report on the divergence between land allocated or permissioned for housing development and the pace at which homes were actually built based on a study of 15 sites confirmed the developer practice of drip-feeding the market. The median build-out

Right to Buy continues to hamper councils' capacity to provide homes as it depletes housing stock and syphons public money out of the system by mandating that sales are made at a significant discount and imposing stringent rules of how much of the resultant cash can be spent on

period was a full 15.5 years, but the slowest development took more than four decades.

Market manipulation of this sort, even if developers are simply acting rationally within this system, rides roughshod over any simplistic law of supply and demand. As a result of this and other distortions of the market for housing, economic modelling indicates, according to the UK Collaborative Centre for Housing Evidence, that "even building 300,000 houses per year in England would only cut house prices by something in the order of 10 per cent over the course of 20 years". A miniscule 0.5 per cent per annum fall in house prices, set against projected annual inflation rates of 2 per cent and long-term wage stagnation, will have no effect on access to housing.

Then we come to the second belief, that the private sector is best placed to deliver new homes for everyone who needs one. Despite the Conservatives' devotional belief in the market, their supporters don't always agree. The Tories' shock loss in the Chesham and Amersham byelection of June 2021 was widely seen as a rebuttal of former housing secretary Robert Jenrick's sweeping planning reform proposals, which rural campaigners excoriated as a "developers' charter". Jenrick's reforms were subsequently ditched by his successor Michael Gove, introducing a "pause" in the legislation that has created a policy vacuum; a vacuum that has been filled with speculation and rumour. Will we get "street votes" giving local people the power to make their own development rules? Will mandatory housing targets for local authorities be scrapped or reinforced? Will land in some areas be exempt from planning permission altogether? Will there be incentives for brownfield sites to encourage urban, as opposed to rural, house-building?

One of the proposed reforms likely to have the greatest impact is the mooted abolition of Section 106, along with the current Community Infrastructure Levy (CIL) and their replacement with a blanket infrastructure levy on developments over a certain size. Since the 1990 Town and Country Planning Act, Section 106 payments having been the flagship instrument for managing this particular variety of "trickle-down" economics. However, there are signs that many housing associations are disillusioned with the sector's reliance on Section 106 and have started to move away from it.

London-based Network Homes, for example, started almost half of its built homes using Section 106 contributions in 2017/18; the following year, that number was down to zero. Over the next two years, it will be just 5 per cent. Network's Matt

Bird has said that "it's not something that has happened by accident. Moving away from Section 106 gives you more control; the number of homes, where they are and the quality of them."

But the capital to build homes must come from somewhere, and the government grants that originally fuelled social house-building have been relentlessly run down. The result is that a social housebuilding sector that embraced divergent motivations, values, funding sources and degrees of independence from commercial pressures is being collapsed into a single, increasingly competitive marketplace. Developers such as British Land are registering their own housing associations, for-profit housing associations are raising investment from the financial industry, and private equity firms are buying up huge tranches of affordable housing. The ultimate prize in this brutally competitive race is land. Housing associations, writes Peter Apps in *Inside Housing* "must now compete in the land market with the big boys and somehow still turn out something which serves a social good".

The notion of land for building on has been eclipsed by the potential of land for speculative investment, as a source of unearned profits, the "economic rent" derived from owning a scarce or exclusive asset. As Josh Ryan-Collins and his co-authors observe in their book *Rethinking the Economics of Land and Housing*, land is "a good that is not subject to the normal laws of market competition". Generally speaking, the supply of land is an absolutely finite quantity, apart from perhaps reclaiming it from the sea or, in the minds of deluded tech plutocrats, by terraforming Mars. As a result, says the book, "the vast majority of ... increases in housing wealth and house prices have come not from increases in building costs ... but from increases in land prices".

Laurie Macfarlane's report for UCL's Institute for Innovation in Public Policy *Is it Time to End Our Obsession with Home Ownership?* notes that "since 1995 alone, the value of Britain's housing stock has increased by £5 trillion, accounting for three-quarters of new household wealth". While that wealth is concomitant upon home ownership, the vast majority of it – a full 90 per cent of transactions – is generated by the trade in existing homes, which because of their dominance set prices for the market overall, including new homes – a situation that privileges anyone already on the 'housing ladder'.

The ultimate irony is that the 40-year campaign to build a "property-owning democracy" has been an outright failure. Home ownership "has been falling for

The ultimate irony is that the 40-year campaign to build a "property-ownning democracy" has been an outright failure. Home ownership has been falling for almost two decades

almost two decades and in June 2021 levels of home ownership were only marginally higher than they were when Right to Buy was introduced in 1980", writes Macfarlane. Just as lower-income households have been progressively bought out, or priced out, of home ownership, the middle-class, especially younger cohorts, have been subjected to a similar, more recent squeeze. Over the past two years, the complicity between business and government has been clear to anyone who cared to look. The plethora of schemes to increase the housing supply and the "democratising" rhetoric around them have, despite being stretched out over a longer timeframe, been similarly damaging.

Where does this leave the 3.8 million people in need of social housing? If the paltry 6,287 affordable social rent homes built in 2019 are any indication, the vast majority of those people are still waiting.

Can local authorities fill the gap? The current regime makes council house-building a Sisyphean task. There are serious constraints – "severe impediments" according to the APSE network of local government officers – on how local authorities can use the capital they raise from Right to Buy sales, in spite of recent changes in response to a 2018 consultation process.

What is strangely difficult to ascertain is what proportion of Right to Buy receipts have been channelled away from local authorities' housebuilding budgets into council debt reduction, subventions to the Treasury and the administrative costs of running the scheme – as mandated by acts of parliament. When then-housing secretary James Brokenshire refused to release this data in 2018, *Inside Housing* used Freedom of Information requests to compile the figures and discovered that in the previous six years, less than half of Right to Buy receipts had been spent on replacement housing. The Treasury took a bit less than 20 per cent – £920 million – while council debt absorbed a whopping £1.1 billion. The end result? "When David Cameron vastly increased Right to Buy discounts in 2012, he promised all additional homes sold would be replaced within three years," reported

Inside Housing. "Since then, councils have sold 63,518 homes and started 15,981 replacements."

Despite the yawning chasm between the number of homes needed and the amount built, it's premature to judge the situation as beyond remedy. Councils are returning to house building, albeit on a small scale, by taking advantage of legislative changes and loopholes, such as the 2018 lifting of the borrowing cap on how much they can raise to fund housing or, delving further back, the 1963 Local Authorities Land Act which empowered councils to develop land. Despite the limited size of individual developments, the reach is impressive, with over 40 per cent of local authorities having started their own housebuilding company. Whether this constitutes "quietly building a housing revolution", as the headline of a late-2019 piece in *The Guardian* suggested, is debatable. The atavistic persistence of Right to Buy means that, despite building new homes, the end result is still a net loss of social housing.

Steve Taylor is a writer and editor who has also worked in innovation with start-ups and accelerators. He recently completed an MRes in Architecture at UEL, led by Anna Minton, where his research involved developing a mapping technique for charting the capital flows through and from Delancey's redevelopment of Elephant and Castle

"Exciting, with all kinds of things happening and really interactive"
Natascha McIntyre Hall, Strategic Developments, Portsmouth City Council.

Join over 600 purpose-driven professionals striving to make a positive impact on places where the common interest is how to make cities that thrive.

The emphasis will be on the spaces between the sessions, with placehacks, workshops, multiple stages, happenings and walking tours, ensuring the community can easily make new connections.

FESTIVAL OF PLACE

6th July 2022
We are back in an exciting new place at BOXPARK Wembley

With its host of diverse street food traders, fun leisure activities to enliven the festival atmosphere, and unique and versatile event space that will enable the festival to thrive. Located in the heart of Wembley Park, one of the largest regeneration projects in Europe, the festival is not to be missed.

For a limited time, get organised with our 2 for 1 offer and bring a colleague for an unmissable day of learning, inspiration and creativity.

Tickets on sale now at www.festivalofplace.co.uk and all enquires to James@thedeveloper.live

Powered by:

Supported by:

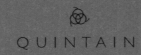

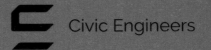

Finland solved homelessness. What's next?

It is the only country in Europe where homelessness has declined. Emma Warren reports on Finland's successful adoption of Housing First

The Jätkäsaari district in southern Helsinki is expected to house 20,000 residents by 2030. Photo: Ilari Näckel/Alamy

Back in 2014, Juha Kaakinen hosted a TED Talk on Finland's remarkable success in reducing numbers of homeless people as well as the country's plans to end homelessness entirely. Towards the end of the talk, Kaakinen reflected on the future. He had six or seven years remaining in his working life as chief executive of non-profit housing developer Y Foundation and he wanted to use that time to ensure real change.

Now Kaakinen is six months away from retirement and Finland is the only country in Europe where homelessness has declined. By 2015, it had fallen by 35 per cent and this year there are fewer than 5,000 homeless people in the country, with two-thirds of those living temporarily with family or friends. The Y Foundation has built or acquired 18,000 apartments since 1985, the majority of which are offered to social housing tenants at affordable rents, with the remaining homes dedicated to previously homeless tenants. Y Foundation is now the fourth largest landlord in the country and is focused on ending homelessness entirely.

"To some extent, of course, I have been involved in making a good change in Finland," says Kaakinen. "There are a lot of younger people who now believe it's possible to reduce or end homelessness. People from other countries too. It's important to see and feel that it's not an impossible dream, but that it requires combining idealistic,

Juha Kaakinen photographed by Kirsi Tuura

The Y Foundation calculates that housing one long-term homeless person saves about €15,000 in other social costs every year. The Finland government calls Housing First a "an economically rational endeavour because it reduces healthcare and social welfare costs"

almost utopian thinking with very pragmatic ways to proceed... It's a Finnish model, but it's not finished yet."

Since the 1980s, the Finnish government has had a progressive approach to housing and, in 2008, officially adopted a national policy of Housing First – an evidence-based approach developed in New York in the early 1990s which offers permanent housing to homeless people as quickly as possible, rather than moving them through levels of emergency or temporary hostels, shelters and short-term transitional housing programmes.

Housing First has proven highly effective, especially when people have high support needs, ending homelessness for at least eight out of ten people. The Y Foundation calculates that housing one long-term homeless person saves about €15,000 in other social costs every year. The Finland government describes Housing First as "an economically rational endeavour, because it reduces healthcare and social welfare costs".

Tuula Tiainen, a senior specialist at Finland's Ministry of the Environment, expands the context. "We have been able to reduce homelessness because we have state-subsidised rental housing, affordable housing and we also have a wide range of social services and a social security system," she says.

With a highly-evolved welfare state and, therefore, low levels of homelessness by European standards, decades of political will in Finland to effect change are matched by a large degree of political consensus.

"Since 2008, we have had eight different governments," says Kaakinen. "We always have coalition governments. All the parties represented in our parliament – at some point they have all been in government – have decided we should continue this national programme to end homelessness. There is a huge political backing for this thing."

What Kaakinen calls a "rather unique" partnership between the state, cities (the mayor of Helsinki recently presented a strategy to end homelessness in the next four years) and NGOs such as the Y Foundation has allowed political backing to turn into realities on the ground.

"This culture of collaboration has been an important element," Kaakinen says, as has the commitment to national leadership on the subject. "We didn't start by launching Housing First as individual projects. We had it as a national policy. We aimed for system change." This meant they had to do something about emergency shelters and hostels, which are now almost non-existent in the country. All short-term temporary emergency housing had to be phased out to put an end to short-term solutions.

"When I look at the advancement of Housing First in other countries," Kaakinen adds, "it often seems to be individual projects, and people speak about upscaling it – and then they say they don't have the housing. Then they are not willing to do anything with the existing shelter and hostel capacity, which is often the main obstacle for ending homelessness."

It hasn't been plain sailing. The Finnish homeless population is mostly single, meaning that small and affordable apartments are required. "On the private housing market, there's a tendency for private investors [to buy these properties] because it's a very good place to park their money to create investment, and that creates a lack of this kind of housing," says Kaakinen. Y Foundation has an ambitious building programme – it plans to complete another 5,500 apartments by 2030 – but it also buys flats from the private market. "Of course, this is difficult," he adds, "when you're competing with private investors who are willing to pay more."

There's another perennial problem. "One obvious obstacle is always the nimby phenomenon," Kaakinen says. "It is not unfamiliar in Finland. It's something we have to tackle all the time."

Tiainen from the Ministry of the Environment agrees. "Cities tried to locate new housing units fairly," she says, "but local resistance was in the beginning very strong. This situation put pressure on dialogue with local schools, daycare centres, old-age homes, shops, etc, and you could say that a new type of environmental, inclusive work model was developed in the process."

It's time-consuming and laborious to work through neighbourhood concerns. Kaakinen describes a development in the city of Espoo, in southern Finland. Part of the block is reserved for young people who need what

Ruoritie Kotka housing units, built by the Y-Foundation in 2016. Photo: Jouni Törmänen

The kitchen in a flat at Ruoritie. Kaakinen says building small and affordable housing is essential. Photo: Jouni Törmänen

The new Helsinki districts of Jatkasaari and Ruoholahti in Finland, pictured in May 2021. This neighbourhood of homes and workplaces is built on what was once a cargo harbour. Photo: Lev Karavanov/Alamy

Kaakinen calls "light support – the kind when you don't have serious social or health issues" – and the rest comprises affordable properties for social housing tenants. It took five years to start building, he says, because of complaints from neighbours. "On a general level, public opinion on the Housing First policy is very favourable but when you get to the level of individual building projects, you still meet a lot of resistance."

While the Ministry of the Environment claims to be moving away from a national model – Tianen says that the focus of homelessness work has been transferred to the municipalities – Kaakinen is resolute that national oversight is essential, noting the government's decision of principle that homelessness should be ended by 2027. "I don't think it's possible to seriously reduce homelessness or end it, as we aim to do, without national leadership at a state level," he says.

Regardless of national machinations, Kaakinen and Y Foundation more broadly are looking towards a post-homeless picture, adapting their work to embrace the present and coming realities of climate change. "We are already looking at the world beyond homelessness," he says. "If we manage to end homelessness by 2027 – which we have to believe because that is the decision and we are working towards it – we have to think about what to do after that. We have started to think how you can combine these things – reducing homelessness and the road to carbon neutral."

Part of that thinking involves what the Y Foundation calls "biodiversity building". Housing is one of the largest contributors to the Finnish carbon footprint, along with transport and food, and the foundation's experimental initiative involves compiling local and international examples of wood-built apartments that promote biodiversity – and allow for food to be grown within the complex – and adapting these examples to the urban environment. Its first wooden apartments were built in Jyväskylä and Kuopio in 2020 and 2021.

"If we manage to end homelessness by 2027, we have to think about what to do after that. We have started to think about how you can combine these things – reducing homelessness and the road to carbon neutral"

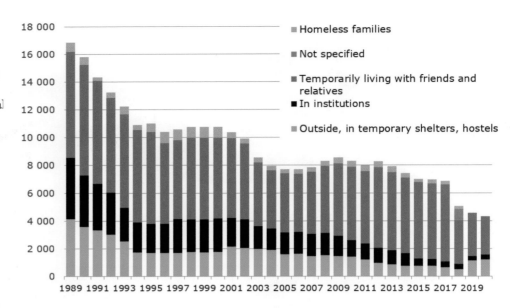

Levels of homelessness in Finland between 1989 and 2019. Y Foundation

Legend:
- Homeless families
- Not specified
- Temporarily living with friends and relatives
- In institutions
- Outside, in temporary shelters, hostels

"It's a very special and unique experiment," says Kaakinen. "The building doesn't have a normal construction basement; it's more or less standing on feet. It touches the ground only lightly, so it doesn't destroy the soil." The whole foundation aims to become carbon neutral by 2035, and that work includes encouraging tenants to reduce their own carbon footprint.

There's plenty for the UK to learn from Kaakinen's decades of experience turning Housing First from a policy aim to a lived reality. He outlines the differences in approach and successes across Britain, noting that Scotland is "doing very well" upscaling Housing First. "England seems to be the black sheep in this respect," he says. "There are good examples, in Manchester for example. What's needed is the political will, the role of the state and wide collaboration. Everyone knows, even in the UK, what needs to be done, and how homelessness could be reduced."

In the 1980s, he worked for the city of Helsinki and visited London to learn how homelessness was dealt with in a big city. "If I went to London now, I would see a lot of similar things that were happening back then," Kaakinen says, noting the specific difficulties presented by the capital's current realities. "The housing market in London is rather unique even by global context," he says, "with people buying apartments where they don't live. The scale of the problem is huge but there are a lot of things that can be done still."

It is, Kaakinen says, a question of imagination. "What would the world look like if there were no homeless people? People smile, they don't believe it's possible, you hear cynical comments. But it's not a law of nature that we will always have homeless people. It's a social problem that can be dealt with – if there is the will to do it."

Emma Warren is an author, editor, journalist and broadcaster with experience in lecturing, workshops and youth work. Her book on the history of a London music venue, Make Some Space: Tuning into Total Refreshment Centre, published in 2019, was named one of MOJO magazine's top 10 books of the year

Jallukka social housing in Helsinki, 2017. Photo: Courtesy of Y-Foundation

Why Berlin's renters want to take back control from private landlords

In Germany, renting rather than buying is the norm, but a referendum saw Berliners vote in favour of expropriating nearly a quarter of a million properties and delivering them into the hands of the city government. Chris Stokel-Walker reports

Berliners protest a decision by Germany's Constitutional Court that ruled a rent cap on Berlin apartments was invalid. Photo: Reuters/Christian Mang/Alamy

Getting a foot on the property ladder is a pipe dream for many people, but in Germany the ladder barely exists. The country boasts the second lowest proportion of people owning their own homes among OECD countries, with less than half of Germans living in a property they own outright. Only Switzerland has a lower figure.

The reasons are multifarious: a high-tax regime on home transfers means people are dissuaded from buying (and selling); there are no reductions in mortgage tax rates for owner-occupiers; and social housing opens its arms broadly and welcomes in people who would be knocked back for being too well-off in other countries. It is partly a legacy of Germany's past; the Second World War and the allies' bombardment of the country meant many Germans were too poor to buy their own homes and the state needed to build new ones to replace those destroyed by bombs. At the peak of this programme in the 1950s, nearly half a million new homes were being built annually that could house renters in West Germany. While the numbers have slowed since, the housing market still differs to anywhere else.

The result? A country where home ownership sits 20 percentage points lower than the United States and United Kingdom, and 30 percentage points below Spain. Renting, rather than buying, is the norm.

But the postwar building boom had unintended consequences. Whereas the UK subsidised housebuilding but set rules so tightly it only allowed the local or national governments – or at a push, non-profits – to build, Germany encouraged private companies to build and then rent out homes. "In Berlin and Germany in general, the structure of the rental market is a lot different from Britain," explains Dan Wilson Craw, deputy director of Generation Rent UK, a British campaign group targeted at improving renters' rights.

Private enterprise built at scale and speed, which is good for putting roofs over people's heads, but bad for renters' rights. Huge

Social housing at Weddingplatz in Berlin-Mitte. Photo: Agencja Fotograficzna Caro/Alamy

In Berlin, one company dominates. Deutsche Wohnen owns more than 113,000 units across the city. It was bought in October by Vonovia, which owns 43,000 units in Berlin. With such power comes the ability to increase rental prices

corporations control thousands of homes at a time, paying little heed to small changes required to make a house a home. The largest private corporate landlord in the United Kingdom is Grainger, which manages more than 9,000 rental properties across the UK. Just one company, Heimstaden, announced it had bought 14,000 homes in Berlin on a single night.

In the German capital, where four in five people reportedly live in rented accommodation, one company dominates: Deutsche Wohnen owns more than 113,000 units across the city. It was bought in October by another company, Vonovia, which owns more properties across Germany – alongside 43,000 in Berlin. With such power comes the ability to increase rental prices. The cost of a Berlin apartment rose two per cent in 2020, at a time when many were absent from work and struggling to make ends meet. The situation has become so bad over the course of decades, with private for-profit companies locking people out of the housing market, that renters have risen up in revolt. The DW und Co Enteignen (Expropriate Deutsche Wohnen and Co) campaign has a lofty goal: expropriating nearly a quarter of a million properties from Deutsche Wohnen and any other private firms that own more than 3,000 apartments each and putting them in the hands of the city government, which will set fairer prices for tenants. The total value of the houses and apartments amounts to billions of Euros.

"The landlords that have all these properties basically speculate with the rent of the people," says Berta Del Ben, a representative of the expropriation campaign. In the decade since Del Ben arrived in Berlin from Italy, rental prices have doubled. "Most of the time, there's no improvement in the houses," says Del Ben. She claims they'll come to paint the doors of the property, but not strip it back to the bare wood. "They're not really engaging with the maintenance of the houses," she says. "The rent is increasing

without the condition of living getting better. And this is pretty common in the entire city."

The goal of the campaign isn't just to win one back for the people. It's to try and reset the Berlin rental market and put it on a new, more prosperous path. The first goal is to get the houses back under state ownership and administrate them independently from the public owners. "If we just ask the state to buy more houses, in 20 years the government will sell them again," worries Del Ben. Many of the properties Deutsche Wohnen now owns were once state-owned properties, bought into the private sector.

City ownership would also help ward off unnecessarily high rent hikes. Del Ben's first apartment in Berlin was one she loved living in, but had to leave when the landlord hiked the price by €400 a month without making any improvements. Del Ben was lucky; she was able to find a suitable new home to live in at the time. But she's conscious that's becoming a vanishingly rare occurrence. "People are really struggling to find a house," she says, "and the problem is finding a house that's affordable." She also dislikes the perception that a decent home in Berlin is treated as a gift from the gods. "It's not," Del Ben says. "It's the minimum. The minimum conditions are so bad that you're happy to have an apartment anyway."

The travails of Berlin's renting population are common conversation in the city's bars and restaurants, claims Del Ben. "Everybody is struggling, especially if you've moved to Berlin, to find a way in the market. Migrants and people who are not German are most discriminated against in the market."

The campaign collected enough signatures for the option to expropriate the properties to be put to a referendum, held in late September 2021. That itself was no mean feat; getting a place on the ballot required 175,000 valid signatures and many non-German citizens were excluded, though they make up a significant share of the city's renting population. More than a quarter of all eligible voters cast a ballot, with 56.4 per cent backing the proposition that properties be expropriated from private mega-landlords.

The referendum was, however, only advisory, and the path ahead is littered with obstacles. The vote came at the same time as an election for the Berlin Senate, and one of the main party leaders has already spoken out against the idea. Senators are exactly the kind of people who have to turn the advisory vote into meaningful action. "It's a long process, but the campaign has a lot of activists," says Del Ben, adding that she's ready for the fight ahead.

Could such action work elsewhere? That is a question on the minds of many

Social housing apartment buildings with garden and mosaic in Graunstrasse, Gesundbrunnen, Berlin. Photo: Eden Breitz/Alamy

The banner from the balcony of an apartment building in Kreuzberg reads "Rent sharks stop". Photo: Wolfram Steinberg/dpa/Alamy

Tenants of flats in Berlin-Friedrichshein demonstrate against gentrification. Photo: Eva Agata Draze/Alamy

"Save social housing – expropriate Deutsche Wohnen" reads the banner on a building at Kottbusser. Credit: Christophe Gateau/dpa/Alamy

of those who rent their properties in other cities around the world, struggling to pay their monthly rents to landlords reticent to improve their properties.

"We're not at the scale of large institutional landlords that would necessarily be the target of a similar campaign here," says Generation Rent UK's Wilson Craw. "But that said, there's quite a good case for bringing private rented stock back into the social sector in a lot of places." Doing something similar, if not exactly the same, would help tackle issues such as homelessness – a problem England spends billions of pounds on each year.

When people become homeless, their local council is tasked with finding them a place to live to rebuild their lives. They're often forced to look to the private sector. "Landlords are able to extract quite a lot of money from councils to do that," says Wilson Craw, pointing to a scarcity of supply and the irony that many people become homeless because they are in rent arrears. "If the council instead had its own larger stock of homes to house people, then they wouldn't be spending these insane sums of money on emergency accommodation," he says.

"Tenants aren't getting a very good deal at present. The homes are often in disrepair, and essentially, a lot of tenants are getting support through the welfare system to pay the rent. Instead of the landlords making a lot of money off the state for a poor service that will often be harmful to a tenant's health, it's better to have the council take those properties back into their ownership, then they can make improvements and invest in the property."

Taking homes back into public ownership could also be beneficial to the country's green agenda. "In many cases these homes will need a lot of upgrading if they're going to meet minimum energy standards in the coming years," says Wilson Craw, pointing to homes in the north and Midlands, where a home could cost £100,000 and need £25,000 to meet minimum energy standards. "They'd rather sell than make the upgrades – so if they're going to sell, they could sell to the council," he says.

Experts admit it's unlikely the Berlin model will map precisely to other countries around the world – but it can do something different. "The expropriation movement is a good way of questioning the extent to which

we need profit-making companies providing housing, and how much we have to rely on them," says Wilson Craw. "It allows us to ask: what can we do to make sure homes are provided with the tenants' – rather than the investors' – interests put first?"

Chris Stokel-Walker is a journalist specialising in digital culture whose work has appeared in Wired, The Economist, Politico, the BBC and The New Scientist. He is the author of two books: YouTubers: How YouTube Shook Up TV and Created a New Generation of Stars (2019); and Tik Tok Boom: China's Dynamite App and the Superpower Race for Social Media (2021)

The Lantern Festival in Kreuzberg, Berlin, is an annual parade in protest against rising rents and gentrification. Photo: Craig Stennett/Alamy

The House of Lords says the government should invest in social housing

The Lords' Built Environment Committee has released a 110-page report that is critical of the government's home ownership schemes such as Help to Buy, and calls for an increase in social housing investment and the reform of Right to Buy. Yustina Baltrusyte reports

Scaffolding is removed from Big Ben as the refurbishment progresses. Photo: VV Shots/iStock

The high cost of rent is preventing people from saving a deposit to buy a home, the House of Lords Built Environment Committee has revealed in Meeting Housing Demand, an 110-page report that delves into the complexity and the challenges of the national housing crisis and what is needed to alleviate this issue.

The report calls on the government to build social homes and reform Right to Buy to help councils replenish social housing stock, while concluding that funding for home-ownership schemes does not provide good value for money. It also expresses concern regarding the £23.4 billion per year of housing benefit spent subsidising private rented accommodation.

The report cites pre-pandemic research that showed 45 per cent of private renters in England already did not have enough savings to pay their rent for more than a month if they lost their job, according to a study from Shelter with YouGov in 2019.

The report concludes that saving up to buy is impossible for many renters, with the average deposit now around £59,000. This is especially so in London where rent accounts for an average of 42 per cent of wages. In 1980, the average working-age family in a private-rented home spent 12 per cent of income on housing; today, excluding London, private renters are spending almost three times this proportion at 32 per cent.

In its written evidence to the committee, the UK Collaborative Centre for Housing Evidence said: "Although it may be the case that preferences have shifted towards renting in the short term as a lifestyle choice, the main constraint on achieving home ownership remains an inability to save the required deposit – a goal that becomes increasingly out of reach if house prices rise faster than savings."

A government survey in 2019 showed that, given free choice, 87 per cent of people would prefer to buy a home rather than rent.

A sign in the window of Yorkshire Building Society: Photo: Alena Kravchenko/iStock

In areas where there is not enough housing, Help to Buy has led to a large increase in house prices with no significant effect on construction numbers. The report is critical of the government's home ownership schemes, which it says are proven to inflate prices by more than their subsidy value

Yet almost half of children today are born to families that are privately renting (49.2 per cent), according to research by Citizens Advice. The report says the number of people renting has doubled from 10 per cent in 2003; there's been a halving of those living in the social-rent sector and a significant decline in home-ownership as growth in house prices outruns growth in wages. In October 2021, the average house price had increased by £24,000 compared to October 2020, shooting up by a staggering 10.2 per cent in just a year to £268,000.

There are significant social consequences to the unaffordability of housing, which most acutely affects key workers and those on low incomes. Toby Lloyd, chair of the No Place Left Behind Commission and an independent housing policy consultant, told the committee: "The private rented sector is by far the most expensive, by far the lowest quality and by far the least popular. It is absolutely the worst possible tenure for almost everybody in it."

The statistics support Lloyd's claim. In 2019-2020, 23 per cent of private rented homes did not meet the government's Decent Homes Standard, amounting to 1.1 million homes. A staggering 28 per cent of private renters receiving housing benefit live in a non-decent home, while 21 per cent of private renters not receiving housing benefit live in non-decent homes. The government has pledged in its Levelling Up white paper to reduce the number of non-decent homes.

"Private rented housing is more likely to be overpriced, in poor condition, overcrowded and have limited forms of redress," the Lords report states, adding that many tenants who would qualify for social housing are now in expensive and overcrowded private rented accommodation with their rent subsidised by housing benefit, costing the government £23.4 billion each year.

The Lords report calls for a shift over time to focus government resources on increasing social housing stock. The proportion of households living in homes for social rent fell from 30 per cent in 1980 to 17 per cent in 2020 and the number of new social rent lettings made in 2019-2020 was 25 per cent lower than in 2012-2013.

According to research conducted by the National Housing Federation and Crisis in 2018, there is a need for 145,000 new affordable houses yearly, of which 90,000 for the next 15 years should be for social rent, 30,000 for affordable rent, and 25,000 for shared ownership homes.

The Lords report encourages the expansion of Build to Rent where it results in a net increase in housing supply, but says this new type of development will need to be closely monitored.

And while it remarks on the significant drop in home ownership, it is emphatic that the government's home ownership schemes do not represent good value for money.

Between 1991 and 2003, around 40 per cent of people whose parents owned their home had become homeowners themselves by the age of 30; this dropped to 25 per cent between 2004 and 2017. For those whose parents were not homeowners, the figure decreased from 19 per cent to 9 per cent.

Christian Hilber, professor of economic geography at the London School of Economics, told the committee that demand-side housing policies, such as the Help to Buy equity loan scheme, tend to increase housing construction only in locations where it is easy to add new housing (such as near the English/Welsh border). However in areas such as Greater London where jobs are located and there is not enough housing, the scheme has led to a large increase in house prices with no significant effect on construction numbers.

The report is critical of the government's home ownership schemes, which it says are proven to inflate prices by more than their subsidy value, having cost around £29 billion in cash terms by 2023. Funding for home ownership schemes do not provide good value for money in the long run; it would be better spent on boosting housing supply.

The Lords report also calls for the reform of Right to Buy. Research from 2017 found that four in ten council homes sold through Right to Buy were now in the private rented sector – 70.6 per cent in Milton Keynes. Anna Minton, reader at the School of Architecture, University of East London, told the committee: "It has long been the case that as we moved from a policy of moving social housing tenants or council housing tenants into the private rented sector, housing benefit

A woman carries her child on a council estate. The report calls on the government to build and invest in social housing and to reform Right to Buy to prevent the further depletion of social housing stock. Photo: track5/iStock

would pay their rents." However, "the local housing allowance no longer covers rents in expensive parts of the country".

Between 2012 and 2018, over 111,000 social rent homes were converted into other forms of affordable housing such as affordable rent, intermediate rent and shared ownership. Homes for affordable rent (at up to 80 per cent of the market rate) were the most common type of new affordable housing being built or acquired in 2019/20, making up 47 per cent of the total." Witnesses questioned how inexpensive "affordable" rentals actually were, particularly in high-cost locations, where 80 per cent of the market rate was still a considerable sum. The Nationwide Foundation stated that "in areas where the housing market is overheated, our concern is that the government's lack of an affordability definition is, in effect, pushing low-income households into poverty."

The Campaign to Protect Rural England said the shortage of social homes due to Right to Buy was particularly acute in rural communities, where the replacement rate

is one new social-rent home built for every eight homes sold.

In March 2021, the government made changes to Right to Buy including extending the time over which councils can spend Right to Buy receipts from three to five years; raising the cap on the percentage cost of new homes councils can fund from Right to Buy receipts from 30 per cent to 40 per cent; allowing receipts to be used for shared ownership and first homes, as well as affordable and social housing; and putting a limit on the use of Right to Buy receipts for purchases.

The Lords paper calls for further Right to Buy amendments to help councils replenish their social housing stock. It says councils should keep more of the proceeds from Right to Buy sales, have a longer time frame to spend the proceeds, and that the circumstances under which tenants can buy their homes should be tightened. The report also states that the government has a poor strategy of announcing additional financing every five or so years. The Local Government

Association commented that this is "extremely inefficient" as it only gives "short term confidence" about grant availability in the future. "A lack of predictability can lead to significant peaks and troughs in delivery, with 'lumpiness' that drives higher unit prices and prevents innovation and investment in the housebuilding supply chain," the LGA stated.

Christopher Pincher, housing minister at the Department for Levelling Up, Housing and Communities, told the committee he was aware of "a significant number of people who would be able to afford a mortgage because the cost of the mortgage repayments would be less than their rent, but [could not] afford the deposit". He said he was exploring "what we can do to make sure that people who want to get on to the housing ladder and who are presently in the private rented sector have opportunities to do so."

Yustina Baltrusyte is publishing and events assistant at The Developer and Festival of Place.

We can save the planet one Environmental Product Declaration at a time

The climate movement has finally found a foothold in the construction sector, with most manufacturers integrating sustainability into their business strategy. But how sustainable are they really?

We need a method to measure the impact of our choices, actions, and claims. One with credible values that replaces complexity and confusion with clarity and confidence. One that simplifies how we talk about and directly considers our climate impact. We need EPDs.

We've been talking about Environmental Product Declarations (EPDs) at Vestre for some time now and last year we published our first catalogue that lists the embodied carbon for every product we make. We were the first furniture manufacturer in the world to do so after we spent a couple of years mapping our products' carbon footprint: interesting, demanding, and rewarding work!

As a Norwegian manufacturer of outdoor furniture, much of this has gone under the radar since we service a tiny niche of the construction sector, both here in the UK and globally. But for us, publishing this information is vital if we're to achieve our ambition of being the most environmentally friendly furniture manufacturer on the planet.

So, what is an EPD and why are we committed to providing this information? An EPD is a transparent, standardised, and verifiable document that reports on a product's environmental impacts and communicates its environmental performance over its lifetime. Absolutely key is that the data is created through a holistic, life-cycle assessment (LCA) and that it's verified by an independent third party. This ensures every EPD is impartial, standardised, accurate, and reliable so that it can be registered and published. Our EPDs conform to EN158054:2012 and are verified by EPD-

"The EPD process requires the collation of detailed data on every aspect of our materials and processes (including raw materials, waste etc) throughout the entire life cycle of resource use, processing, manufacturing, distribution, use, and end of life (recycling)"

Norge. An EPD essentially details a product's carbon footprint (or Global Warming Potential) and additional environmental impacts of production, such as acidification, ozone depletion, and water consumption.

The process requires the collation of detailed data on every aspect of our materials and processes (including raw materials, waste etc) throughout the entire life cycle of resource use, processing, manufacturing, distribution, use, and end of life (recycling). Through this standard format, an EPD provides transparent information on key environmental impacts, and allows scrutiny of purported "sustainable" or low-carbon products; it also enables the receipt of credits for green building standards and regulations, such as LEED and BREEAM.

The use of EPDs supports the reduction of carbon emissions as it enables direct comparison of the impacts of any number of products in order to select those with the least impact. EPDs are much like the nutritional values found on food labels. They don't promise health benefits, but they provide critical data at a glance.

We know this information fully supports our marketing claims (including that of being the world's most sustainable furniture manufacturer) and will bring about the informed specification and ultimate purchasing of our products. From a client and procurement perspective, EPDs make it easier to specify environmentally superior products. We hope that soon, all stakeholders of a construction project will demand EPDs as a matter of course.

We started publicly sharing our EPD

re street furniture

values at the Stockholm Furniture Fair in 2020. Next to each piece of furniture, display boards informed visitors of the carbon emissions from each product's life cycle: for instance, our FOLK bench, designed by Swedish studio Front, has a carbon footprint of 3.75kg of carbon dioxide per year, assuming the product remains in use for 30 years. This focus on a product's life is critical. All of our products come with a lifetime guarantee

"While product longevity has been a core value of ours since our inception 75 years ago, with the advent of EPDs and carbon accounting, we can finally calculate the financial and environmental upside from choosing a product that lasts decades longer than the alternative"

against rust. By manufacturing for life, we reduce our energy consumption and environmental impact by a huge amount.

While product longevity has been a core value of ours since our inception 75 years ago, only now can we measure the impact of this approach. With the advent of EPDs and carbon accounting, we can finally calculate the financial and environmental upside from choosing a product that lasts decades longer than the alternative. By understanding total emissions, both embodied and in-use, our customers are in a better position to review the impact of our products in terms of both emissions and price from a lifecycle perspective (and they're intrinsically linked).

While preparing our EPDs, we realised something: by having an honest look in the mirror – turning over every stone, measuring and counting everything – we became a better business. Even more aware of our place in the world and accountable for our impact. We uncovered new and better ways to care for our clients and community, and we use our EPD insights to make informed choices on which materials to use, where to source them, and how to

process them. These metrics prove we are making the world a little better every day.

As we gain momentum as a business, the more we learn about the impact of everything we do, the more informed choices we can make, the better we become. And we gladly share what we have learned so far through our EPD journey. We believe having metrics on a product's carbon footprint should be as common as nutritional value labels on food. So that then, everyone has the data needed to make informed choices for a healthy planet.

Just how serious is the government about modern methods of construction?

Last October the government finally published its 202-page Heat and Buildings strategy, with one glaring omission: modern methods of construction. How close are factory-built homes to making the breakthrough? asks James Wilmore

Designed by ZED PODS, Hope Rise is a net zero carbon development of 11 homes for vulnerable young people at risk of homelessness. The modules are 90% factory built and were erected in five days on stilts above an existing car park in Bristol. Photo: Courtesy of ZED PODS

Heralded as the strategy that will decarbonise UK homes and buildings as the country moves towards net zero 2050, the Heat and Buildings Strategy was published by the Department for Business, Energy & Industrial Strategy in October 2021.

In its 202 pages, there were tub-thumping mentions of Britain's "green industrial revolution" and the country as a "global leader" for green technologies. But at least one thing was missing.

The long-awaited document laying out the transition to more energy-efficient buildings failed to highlight how building new homes could benefit from modern methods of construction (MMC) – the catch-all term for everything from factory-built homes and modular construction to onsite technology such as drones and exoskeletons.

The omission is odd. For some time the MMC sector has been talking up and demonstrating its credentials when it comes to tackling the climate emergency and the housing crisis. The energy-efficient buildings being produced – at a faster pace than a traditional build and in the controlled environment of a factory – tick a lot of boxes. The use of often more eco-friendly materials such as timber is another plus.

How any of this failed to get a proper mention is bizarre. Aside from one fleeting reference to the "testing of modular and offsite retrofit and refurbishment solutions", there was nothing said in the context of new homes. One source described the omission as "bonkers".

Offsite home manufacturers are perplexed. Dave Sheridan, executive chairman of Ilke Homes, says the failure to recognise MMC is "quite frustrating". He adds: "We can accelerate the delivery of net zero homes as we've got proven solutions. I don't lose sleep over it but it's an opportunity missed."

The government's blindspot has not, however, changed Ilke Homes' strategy. It is pioneering a concept known as Ilke Zero, part of a commitment to create whole zero carbon communities by 2030. The company claims that anyone living in an Ilke Zero home will pay nothing for their energy.

Sheridan says he is already seeing interest from clients and that around 400 homes in its 3,500-home pipeline will adopt the Ilke Zero concept.

Other modular housing producers are also pushing their net zero credentials. Legal & General boasts that its modular flats and family homes already have an Energy Performance Certificate rating of A and is eyeing its first net zero carbon scheme. The wider L&G group has made a pledge to be operationally net zero by 2030.

The Goldman Sachs-backed TopHat,

"We would like to see the government fast-track planning for modular construction, treating modular as its own product with its own distinct characteristics and control, and better access to land for volumetric housing"

meanwhile, says its homes have around 3.7 per cent the embodied carbon of a traditional home, partly due to their use of timber. The firm also offers what it calls a "net zero" home.

At the same time, large traditional housebuilders – which the modular firms are hoping to catch up with – are flashing their eco credentials too.

Barratt, the UK's biggest housebuilder, launched its Z House concept in October, claiming it would be the first new home in the country built by a major housebuilder to go beyond the new Future Homes Standard. The product features closed panel timber frames and "highly insulated" cladding as well as using technology such as air source heat pumps, electric vehicle charging points, photovoltaic solar panels and battery storage.

Meanwhile at rival Countryside last month, a senior executive declared that it was the UK's "leading MMC provider", aiming for a target of 20,000 new homes using MMC – around 50 per cent of its output – by the middle of the decade.

Clearly there is no shortage of ambition within the sector. But the government's failure to properly get to grips with MMC in some of its thinking is apparent elsewhere.

In general, central government and its agencies have been supportive, including financially. Homes England made an ultimatum that strategic partners on its Affordable Homes Programme must adopt at least 25 per cent MMC on their schemes. The agency has also pumped money into Ilke Homes, lending it £30 million in 2019 and a further £30 million in 2021.

But there is also evidence that Homes England is not keeping track. In December, the agency admitted it was not collecting data on how many homes are being built using MMC. Chief executive Peter Denton told MPs that key performance indicators around MMC were harder to track and a new strategy would look to address this.

On top of this, a £10 million MMC Taskforce, announced in the March 2021 Budget, has so far failed to materialise.

All these knocks have done nothing to dampen the industry's ambition. But it is perhaps timely that five of the MMC sector's biggest players have now launched their own trade group, Make UK Modular, to push their case to government.

On the Heat and Buildings Strategy, Make UK Modular's head, Steve Cole, says: "Obviously we would have liked to have seen MMC mentioned properly, given that it has an integral role to play. But with the government committing £10 million to the MMC Taskforce, it might be they see this coming through in that area of work."

Cole is also mindful of the fact that there is a certain onus on the sector to monitor its own output. "I'd be reluctant to criticise the government on that when we don't have the statistics," he says.

But one thing Cole would like to see from government is fast-track planning for modular construction. "We would like to see something that treats modular as its own product with its own distinct characteristics and control, and better access to land for volumetric housing," he says.

Cole also thinks the government could give more financial reassurance to the sector. "We would like to work with government so the industry is really underpinned by a robust financial and borrowing system with the government lender of last resort or guarantee," he says. "Providing that sort of underpinning would be useful in what is still quite a nascent industry."

While there's plenty of ambitious talk from offsite players, there remains a feeling that MMC has yet to fulfil its potential. Financially, the big players are still in start-up mode, with Ilke Homes, L&G and TopHat all reporting major annual losses in their most recent available accounts.

Scale is required to make the breakthrough. Among those trying to crack the scale conundrum are housing associations, with two eye-catching initiatives.

The Offsite Homes Alliance (OSHA) is a group of 23 predominantly north of England-based housing associations, which have joined forces to share knowledge and procure MMC homes collectively. The group's affiliated partners include the Greater Manchester Combined Authority and Homes England.

OSHA is preparing to launch a £4 billion framework with around 15 offsite housing firms expected to be signed up. Its 23 members have a combined total development pipeline of 10,000 homes a year though not all of these will be MMC homes. Mike Ormesher, OSHA's project director, says trailblazer sites are being developed and

Commissioned by Nottingham City Homes, the NCH2050 Homes will retrofit 150 existing homes with new pre-fabricated external envelopes

At NCH2050, Melius Homes removed gas boilers, installed heat pumps and added a solar photovoltaic system with battery storage

Crescent of factory-built townhouses designed by architect ShedKM at Smith's Dock, in North Shields, North Tyneside for Urban Splash.
Photo: Washington Imaging/Alamy

Construction of a modular home at New Islington in Manchester. Photo: Courtesy of Make UK Modular

around 1,500 homes are likely to be delivered in the year. But he expects this to scale up significantly in the next few years. "We have Great Places, Guinness and Yorkshire Housing and the bulk of the homes will be with those organisations," he says. "Therefore we should have a significant chunk of homes to go for in the next 12 to 24 months."

So can OSHA be a game changer? "There are around 900 registered providers out there that want to build homes," says Ormesher. "The model they require is a sustainable, maintenance-free product so they don't have to keep retrofitting. They see that that can come from the MMC offsite sector because it's a more controlled way of doing things.

"We're only a small group, but with a big ambition and it is most definitely the right thing to do. How we move forward remains to be seen, but at the moment, we're getting a very strong stakeholder interest from a number of different areas of the sector."

Ormersher believes OSHA has the potential to become national, but he says "if that doesn't happen there's no reason that others can't follow the model we have".

Working on a similar model to OSHA, but one step ahead, is the Building Better initiative, which is backed by the National Housing Federation. It launched a £600 million framework in July with Ilke Homes, Impact Modular and TopHat as chosen suppliers. The firms are expected to deliver at least 800 modular homes by 2026 as part of the framework, with a second framework due to be launched next spring.

Inside Legal & General's 550,000 sq ft factory for homes in Sherburn-in-Elmet, near Leeds. Photo: Courtesy of Make UK Modular

> "There are around 900 registered providers out there that want to build homes. They require a sustainable, maintenance-free product so they don't have to keep retrofitting. That can come from the MMC offsite sector because it's a more controlled way of doing things"

Avril Roberts, development project manager at London-based housing association RHP Group, which is part of Building Better, says the initiative is helping realise its ambitions on MMC. "RHP has been keen on MMC for a long time but we haven't really been able to deliver it," she says. "Building Better makes it much more accessible. When you are approaching suppliers to procure 800 homes instead of 10, it's easier." RHP has around 70 homes going through the framework.

"What Building Better has shown is that you can go to a manufacturer and say: can you build this for us? That was the struggle before. It's not just the framework, there's also the innovation side of it, where we are talking to manufacturers about how they can improve their products."

But Roberts acknowledges that MMC will still be seen as a risk until it can be proven long term. "For housing associations and developing authorities, it's a risk in terms of the unknown," she says. "For their maintenance teams, they don't know how they're going to maintain it and they don't know what's in there."

Safety is an issue that continues to dog the MMC sector. While firms talk up their order books, it has emerged that serious worries about remain among fire chiefs and one of the UK's biggest insurance companies. In January, as housing secretary Michael Gove announced new efforts to get to grips with the post-Grenfell building safety crisis, a cross-peer parliamentary report emerged on housing supply. Buried in its footnotes are links to evidence supplied by among others the London Fire Brigade and National Fire Chiefs Council (NFCC), and insurance giant Zurich.

And while new-build initiatives are well and good, the fact is that properly reaching net zero will mean retrofitting existing housing stock. So where does MMC fit into that equation? Ilke's boss believes there is still an opportunity. "We are building new homes, but we are keen that any technology that we help engineer can be retrofitted," says Sheridan. "We have one eye on the retrofit market."

Make UK Modular's membership – which includes Ilke – can be involved in retrofit. "It's not something in the immediate term that our membership is focused on, but they will have a role to play," Cole says. "The housing crisis is twofold: a crisis of supply and quality of existing stock. I'm sure there is a role modular can play in addressing quality of the existing stock. The trick for government is not taking their eye off one of those balls."

One retrofit project using MMC is in Nottingham. The NCH2050 Homes project, touted as the first of its kind in the UK, used the Energiesprong approach, first pioneered in the Netherlands. It involves using MMC techniques to retrofit whole homes to make them more energy efficient. The scheme was showcased at COP26 in Glasgow.

If the government is to get anywhere near its 300,000 homes a year target by the middle of the decade, and achieve net zero, MMC will need to be a significant part of the mix. But as with anything new in the construction industry, there is caution and a reluctance to move away from tried and tested formulas. Yet with so many factors and initiatives coalescing, now is the perfect time for MMC manufacturers to step up to the plate.

Make UK Modular has said its members have the capacity to deliver 75,000 modular homes by the end of the decade.

"We'd like to see that level of ambition from the government," says Cold. "And it makes sense given the shortfall of new homes in this country is around about 100,000 anyway. We're looking for modular to make up a substantial part of that."

James Wilmore is a journalist and editor whose work has appeared in Inside Housing, Social Housing, Construction News and Planning. Wilmore is the founding editor of independent newsletter Modular Monitor which covers news in the MMC sector

Thanks to our supporters for making independent journalism possible

With your help, we commission reporters and photographers to bring you fresh insight into the issues facing the development of urban places

Thanks to our proud supporters, we are able to publish campaigning journalism and podcasts, and produce challenging independent events featuring fresh and expert voices, providing free tickets to small charities, outreach and community groups. Become an organisation or individual member to support our work and you'll receive every issue of our uncommonly beautiful print edition of *The Developer* and free access to all Festival of Place events, including the all-access in-person pass to the annual summit and digital access to our annual programme and library of Festival talks. To find out more, visit www.thedeveloper.live, email subscriptions@thedeveloper.live or call 020 3326 7238

Broadoak
Civic Engineers
Commonplace
David Chipperfield Architects
EPR
Homes England
HTA Design
LDA Design
LocatED
LUC
Make
Poplar HARCA
Quintain
Stride Treglown
Sustrans
Tibbalds
Vestre

Local authorities should lead on the energy retrofit of social housing

Do councils have the skills and resources they need? By Pooja Agrawal and Ben Hockman of Public Practice

Insulate Britain protesters glued themselves to the road and blocked Wormwood Street and Bishopsgate, close to Liverpool Street Station, on 25 October, 2021. The protesters are demanding that the government insulates all social housing by 2025, and takes responsibility for ensuring all homes in the UK are more energy-efficient by 2030, as part of wider climate change and decarbonisation targets. Photo: Vuk Valcic/Alamy

In the last few years, around 300 local authorities have declared a climate emergency – that's 74 per cent of all local authorities in the UK. In addition, a number of councils have pledged to reach net zero carbon by 2030, a more ambitious timeline than the national target. Authorities are taking a number of different routes, including decarbonising transport, investing in green space and nature, adapting their waste management and, of course, retrofitting housing stock.

The built environment is responsible for 39 per cent of energy-related carbon emissions according to the UK Green Building Council and the role of housing is even more significant within the sector. According to the LETI Climate Emergency Retrofit Guide, of all the operational emissions that come from buildings in the UK, 69 per cent come from energy use in the domestic stock which alone is responsible for 18 per cent of our annual national emissions.

Retrofitting buildings is considered to be a key solution to tackling this issue and is broadly defined as the process of improving a property's efficiency to reduce energy consumption. With UK households facing a 54% rise in energy bills, the issue is gaining national attention. Retrofitting can include the installation of a new building technology such as a heating system or replacing an existing fabric such as insulation or single glazing. Deep retrofitting of the building fabric and the inclusion of a heat pump can reduce the average energy demand of a home by up to 75 per cent, according to LETI. Retrofitting is therefore an important part of the puzzle in meeting the government's target to achieve net zero by 2050.

The biggest challenges are scale and cost. Who is going to pay for retrofitting

North London Housing Coop retrofitted this 1980s Kentish Town social housing block of 15 flats in 2019 to EnerPHit standards, a Passivhaus certification for retrofits

Who is going to pay for retrofitting with no immediate return on investment? Who is going to bring together the range of stakeholders – from a construction industry not ready to deliver at scale to residents who will need to deal with the disruption?

with no immediate return on investment? Who is going to bring together the range of stakeholders – from a construction industry not ready to deliver at scale to residents who will need to deal with the disruption? Who will make the argument for the wider social value that retrofitting can bring, such as tackling fuel poverty, improving health and wellbeing and creating employment opportunities?

Local authorities have an opportunity to lead the way and bring the market, industry and residents with them on the road to net zero. But they face significant challenges to delivering. Mark Atherton, director of environment at Greater Manchester Combined Authority, says retrofitting needs to be tackled as a whole country "at a huge scale – a scale that hasn't really been seen before in any other enterprise".

For local authorities, retrofitting can be a political minefield. Councils need to make tough decisions, for example diverting funding from new housing and thus compromising on ambitious housing targets set by national government. There is a valid question about what will create a greater impact, investing in new zero-carbon buildings or futureproofing existing homes?

Estate retrofitting can be seen as another form of estate regeneration where existing communities may be displaced or decanted. Conversations around the climate emergency can also stoke culture wars – low traffic neighbourhoods are just one example of how debates on the future of mobility can divide communities.

The London Borough of Camden is one local authority taking its first steps. Council leader Georgia Gould sees retrofitting as a "triple win" of job creation, dealing with climate crisis and tackling fuel poverty. Gould strongly believes in bringing residents into the strategic conversations in order to build coalition over urgent issues.

In July 2019, Camden organised the UK's first citizen's assembly on the climate

crisis and, over three sessions, developed proposals based on evidence from scientists, environmentalists and community energy practitioners. A number of community-led initiatives were born such as community greening, allotments, a library of things and local repair shops. In themselves these could be seen as small measures but the larger picture, Gould believes, is that they can build a coalition of community-led change linking the climate crisis to other policy areas such as retrofitting.

In September 2020, Camden Council set up a Renewal Commission with University College of London's Institute of Innovation and Public Purpose. Co-chaired by Gould and the institute's founding director, Mariana Mazzucato, they brought together residents, businesses, activists, academics and organisational leaders to take a "mission-led" approach to build a more equal and sustainable society post-pandemic. The mission-led approach is radical. It involves the conversation moving away from who does what within the status quo and towards a shared understanding of collective problems that can be worked on together. One of the four missions set out by the commission is that "by 2030, Camden's estates and their neighbourhoods are healthy, sustainable and unlock creativity" for which a key outcome is delivering a retrofit programme.

Finding the balance between a top-down and a grassroots approach is always tricky. Camden is taking a mission-led approach to bringing businesses, residents, officers and politicians together.

After a decade of austerity, with local authorities experiencing 38 per cent cuts in funding from national government and more recently with the impact of the pandemic, it is no secret that they are struggling financially. As clear as the long-term benefits of retrofitting may be, paying for work that doesn't have an income or revenue stream attached to it means finding new ways to secure funding. It is estimated that for social housing, the cost of decarbonising all homes is likely to be in the region of £104 billion by 2050, according to *Inside Housing*.

Camden completed a detailed analysis of its stock, which might seem an obvious starting point, but it's surprising how few councils have the necessary data on their housing portfolios. Camden owns 100,000 homes – about a third of the borough's housing stock – of which around half are in buildings over 100 years old and three-quarters are flats. This may not be run of the mill for most authorities; Camden has a legacy of a progressive approach to public housing in the mid-late 20th century. Across the country, post-war housing is often

Councils are looking to The Netherlands for innovative funding models where tenants contribute to the cost of retrofit, such as Energiesprong and "warm rent". Photo: Евгений Вершинин/Alamy

coming to the end of its life and is in need of substantial investment.

From Camden's analysis it estimates that to make its existing housing stock genuinely zero carbon would require £706 million of investment. It currently has £91 million set aside and a huge gap to fill. David Burns, the council's director of economy, regeneration and skills, believes this number is probably an underestimate given the post-Brexit increased labour and construction material costs.

Looking to national government for grant funding is inevitable. In August 2021, the Department of Business, Energy and Industrial Strategy announced the Social Housing Decarbonisation Fund, releasing £160 million of cash to enhance the energy efficiency of socially rented homes – a drop in the ocean in terms of the total sum required. Burns explains that there is also a huge amount of uncertainty in the industry and local government around the government's plans and long-term approach on the back of its sudden scrapping of the Green Homes Grant (small grants for private households to install low carbon heating and insulation) in March 2021 without explanation.

Authorities will need to look beyond national government grants for solutions, and councils are looking to the Netherlands for inspiration. "Warm rents" is an approach commonly used there, where landlords charge higher rents to help cover the cost of investment while the tenant saves money on energy bills. At a larger scale, another model is Energiesprong, where a deep retrofit is financed by tenants paying an energy service plan over 30 years, with residents keeping the same cost of living. Nottingham City Homes was the first housing association in the UK to pilot net-zero retrofits of social housing using the Energiesprong approach on a pilot scheme with Melius Homes at a maximum tenant cost of £330 per year.

Camden is also exploring PFI to share the risk. There are innovative financers such as Bankers Without Boundaries, interested in environmental and social impact, however

"Warm rents" is an approach commonly used in the Netherlands, where landlords charge higher rents to help cover the cost of investment while the tenant saves money on energy bills

there is not enough proven evidence of the returns on such schemes at the moment and private institutions are nervous about the risk and initial investment required.

Authorities are, therefore, in situation where they need proof of concept but also investment to prove the concept. Camden is now in the process of delivering pilot schemes on the ground, having done the early work of mapping stock, scoping the budget and looking at financial opportunities. But it's at scale that one is able to garner investment, bring the industry on board and make a real impact. Burns believes that, despite some nervousness about authorities leading the way (chastened by the collapse of Croydon Council's housebuilding company Brick By Brick) delivering the programme in-house is the way forward.

Funding isn't the only challenge. Post-Brexit, there are concerns regarding the lack of labour and skills. Gould reckons that based on the workforce available, there is only the capacity to retrofit one borough in London. But Camden sees retrofitting as an opportunity to support local education providers and ensure local residents are trained to take those jobs. Camden has undertaken a scoping study with consultants to create a framework to align training and employment support within the programme of retrofit capital works.

Do authorities have the in-house capacity and skills they need? From Public Practice's latest round of recruitment, we are seeing increased demand from authorities seeking the housing, sustainability and technical expertise to coordinate the delivery of a retrofitting programme. Public Practice associate Rafe Bertram produced a job template for a sustainability facilitator after finding authorities struggle even at this first step of recruitment.

Over the years, Camden has worked with Public Practice to bring expertise in areas such as urban design and regeneration in-house. One of our associates, Alastair Crockett, previously an associate at Níall McLaughlin Architects, brought his design skills to Camden's internal retrofitting working-group. Along with the need to move beyond internal siloed ways of working, Crockett says authorities need to work in a more collaborative way. Climate change does not recognise administrative boundaries.

Camden is taking an in-house, multidisciplinary, place-based approach to retrofitting, working with neighbouring boroughs Islington and Haringey as part of the West London Alliance, to create investable propositions at scale to appeal to private-sector investors, including green finance models.

The Energiesprong pilot project in Nottingham retrofitted 10 homes

Retrofitting existing homes can be seen as a radical way of tackling systemic issues in a practical way. The road ahead is clearly not going to be easy but this is a shared challenge that is urgent and needs to be collectively bought into by all members of society.

A colossal amount of money is required, and though we need central government to invest more in retrofitting grant programmes, we also need to be innovative in finding new models for funding and partnerships. Mazzucato believes that in 2022 we need to see the birth of a new social contract, "one which puts purpose at the centre of public private partnerships so that investment decisions are not driven by private profit but are guided by co-investment of both public and private actors towards the common good," she writes in *The Wired World*. To achieve their goal of net-zero by 2030, local authorities need the confidence, capacity and multidisciplinary skills to test new approaches, new financial models and new partnerships to deliver a retrofitting programme at scale for the common good.

Pooja Agrawal and Ben Hockman are chief executive and programme manager at Public Practice, a not-for-profit social enterprise with a mission to improve the quality, equality and sustainability of places, primarily through placing mid-career level built environment practitioners (associates) looking for a career change into public sector organisations

Although not strictly an energy-efficiency project, Camden Council's former offices have been transformed into The Standard, a five-star hotel completed by architect Orms with interior designer Shawn Hausman and interior architect Archer Humphryes, proof positive that where there's a will (and financial backing), there's a way forward for council-owned buildings. Photo: SMPNEWS/Alamy

There's not enough water in Cambridge

Drought is a sword of Damocles dangling over Cambridge's local plan and the wider Oxford-Cambridge arc. If the government and water industry fail to act, housebuilding can't go ahead, writes Christine Murray

A local person walks along Osprey Drive past new-build houses and apartment blocks in Trumpington Meadows, Cambridge.
Photo: Georgina Scott/Alamy

To say there's a water crisis in UK property is not hyperbole. Be it filthy, in short supply or at risk of flooding, the state of England's water is not only a threat to human health, it's undermining the twin ambitions to build homes and build back better.

In districts across England, planning applications are on hold, with tens of thousands of homes in limbo and local plans in jeopardy as embargoes on development follow notices from Natural England. In southern England, a moratorium on planning was enacted to protect the Sussex North Water Supply Zone in the districts of Horsham, Crawley and Chichester and South Downs National Park. Future applications are required to demonstrate water neutrality – that they do not increase pressure on water resources.

Yet even where Natural England has not triggered a planning moratorium, water is a major threat to future development. In the Oxford-Cambridge Arc, drought is a sword of Damocles dangling over its local plan. The arc is located in the most water-stressed region in the UK, and increasingly prone to water shortages with global heating, putting pressure on water use for homes, farming and businesses. Independent studies commissioned by Cambridge City Council have shown that the current level of water abstraction from the chalk aquifer is unsustainable.

The Greater Cambridge Local Plan is unequivocal: "This can only happen if further work is done to address current water supply issues ... If the water industry and central government do not take action, the number of new homes may need to be reduced."

"Water is an absolute critical issue for the local plan," says Katie Thornburrow, executive councillor for planning policy and transport at Cambridge City Council. "There is no capacity to increase groundwater abstraction from the chalk aquifer. Development levels may have to be capped to avoid unacceptable harm to the environment, including the region's important chalk streams. We have been clear that we will not allow housebuilding to go ahead if the only way to supply it with water would result in further environmental damage to the chalk aquifer."

"Water is a real threat to the sustainable growth of Cambridge," says Tom Holbrook, director of 5th Studio, an architecture practice that undertook the Oxford-Milton Keynes-Cambridge Corridor study for the National Infrastructure Commission. "Anglian Water is planning a new reservoir, but it extracts the same water from the Ouse catchment – and that's already in trouble."

Holbrook says the problem is too severe

to be addressed by the design of new homes. "No amount of restrictors on taps or bricks in cisterns is going to address the level of scarcity," he says, adding that the issue needs tackling at the regional scale but "there aren't the right strategic planning frameworks, and the water company areas fragment the area in an unhelpful way in relation to watersheds."

Holbrook has been arguing for a 100-mile new national park that would convey water from the Derwent-Trent catchment. This major project, which assembles a number of existing proposals into a larger whole over time, would restore the derelict Banbury arm of the Grand Union Canal, and create a "continuous riverine landscape" from the Cherwell to the Cam, with a new Bedford and Milton Keynes waterway linking the Grand Union Canal to the Ouse.

"It would need proper funding that will never come just 'from the market' – but requires partnership with local and national government," Holbrook says.

Given the Oxford-Cambridge Arc has been touted since 2003 as a flagship government project, you would think that government funding for water infrastructure would be a no-brainer, with prime minister Boris Johnson having bolstered the arc as "a compelling 'front door' for international investors".

But there is speculation that, under the new levelling up agenda, government priorities have shifted away from Ox-Cam, despite the once fevered rhetoric.

On future investment, an Environment Agency spokesperson said: "As we look to the next round of water resources management plans early next year, water companies again will be taking some big decisions around investments in their infrastructure. The planned growth in Ox-Cam will feature in this, and the plans will ensure there is enough water available."

David Rogers, professor of ecology at the University of Oxford has written that pipeline plans to pump water to Cambridge to enable housebuilding may trigger other unintended consequences. Rogers told the *Cambridge*

Independent, "Pumping water into the region or building huge new reservoirs is an engineering solution. But the only reason you have to do this is because you are building too many new houses in the area for the natural resources to cope with. And while you may be able to solve water shortages through engineering, the problem of all the extra sewage a million homes will create is not being addressed. Where will the sewage go?"

Cambridge isn't the only city region with sewage and water problems undermining plans. Since 2019, 10 of England's local planning authorities (LPAs) have issued planning moratoriums due to polluted rivers with high nitrate levels after receiving advice from Natural England.

Such moratoriums have hit Herefordshire Council in the catchments of the River Wye and River Lugg (2019), the Solent region (2019), Kent in the Stour Valley catchment (July 2020), South Somerset District, Sedgemoor District, Mendip District, Somerset West and Taunton Councils' Somerset Levels and Moors (August 2020), and Cornwall Council's River Camel (April 2021).

Research by Savills has suggested 10 per cent of LPAs in England have been affected, which will cause a 50-70 per cent drop in the volume of new homes delivered.

An excess of nitrate in rivers is caused by intensive agriculture in combination with the sewage crisis. In 2020, not a single river in England was considered to be in good health. Farms in England are feared to have been left unregulated by a lack of inspection and enforcement. The Environment Agency recently announced it would hire an additional 50 new farm inspectors in addition to the existing staff of 28 – a total of 78 staff charged with inspecting some 192,000 English farms. As for enforcement, not one of the 243 violations documented by the Environment Agency has been prosecuted or fined since 2018.

A leaked report by the Environment Agency in early 2020 revealed that fertiliser spread on farms contained dangerous chemicals including E-Coli, microplastics, salmonella, persistent organic pollutants and the antimicrobial triclosan, which scientists believe may cause antibiotic resistance. A 2018 study of the River Axe in Somerset by the Environment Agency found that half of all the local farmers were polluting the river.

Sewage overflows from crumbling water infrastructure compound the nitrate problem, an issue that recently ignited public anger. Sewage pollution in British seas has increased by 88 per cent, according to a 2021 Surfers against Sewage water quality report.

All these water problems, and we

A sign advertising a new development in a field outside Cambridge. Photo: Georgina Scott/Alamy

Eco-homes in Elsmbrook, Bicester, in the Ox-Cam arc, a 6,000-home project to build an eco-town. Photo: Oxfordshire LEP

haven't event addressed a well-known risk to property in the UK: flooding, with one in ten new homes built in England at risk. Environment Agency inspectors last year found that more than 1,000 privately owned flood defences were classed as in a poor or very poor condition, threatening places such as Sheffield and Rochdale. Nearly a third of all "high consequence" flood defences are owned privately.

Surface flooding is a sewage problem. Floods last summer in Walthamstow, east London, had residents complaining about signs of raw sewage in the streets and inside flooded homes after the drains were overwhelmed by a sudden July downpour. In October, homes and streets in Cumbria were flooded with sewage as overflows struck at 14 sites along the coast.

Taken together, it's perhaps unsurprising that the water crisis is raising hairs on the arms of property investors as they seek sites for socially responsible ESG (Environmental, Social and Governance) investment.

Alexandra Notay, placemaking and investment director for PfP Capital says: "Investors are looking more closely at all ESG factors. The implication of flooding has always been a risk factor but it's being scrutinised more than ever before."

Notay says developers are seeing increased costs due to flood risk, with a growing expectation by councils to provide dry escape routes, while also restricting uses on the ground and lower-ground floors due to flood-risk, increasing the pressure to build higher. She says flood risk assessments can change the value of land overnight – and flooding itself is unpredictable. While flood risk has traditionally been based on historical records, she says: "We now know it's not the new builds on the floodplain that tend to flood, but adjacent neighbourhoods that have never flooded."

The UK water crisis comes as water companies are facing a growing public backlash, with everyone from singer Bob Geldof to the leader of Portsmouth City Council joining the call for change and threatening actions such as a boycott on payment of water bills. Meanwhile, water industry regulator Ofwat has raised alarm over the financial health of Southern Water, Yorkshire Water and SES Water, casting doubt on whether they will be able to improve their environmental performance.

It is perverse to see the water industry undermine planning, given their shared history. Access to clean water and sanitation is the most basic of development ambitions as the sixth UN Sustainable Development goal. It seems inconceivable that housebuilding in England could be hamstrung by an inability to provide decent water services, yet there it is.

Christine Murray is the founder and Editor-in-Chief of The Developer, and Director of its annual event, Festival of Place. An award-winning writer, editor and architecture critic, Murray is the former Editor-in-Chief of The Architectural Review and The Architects' Journal, where she founded the Women in Architecture Awards (now W Awards).

"Investors are looking more closely at all ESG factors. The implication of flooding has always been a risk factor, but it's being scrutinised more than ever before"

Hundreds of people gathered on Port Meadow, Oxford on 22 January, 2022 to protest against sewage being released into the River Thames.
Photo: Elly Godfroy/Alamy

Whole streets of family homes are being converted into Houses in Multiple Occupancy

Where is the statutory oversight? Emma Warren reports on the HMO landlords buying up houses to create bedsit "poverty traps" designated as exempt accommodation

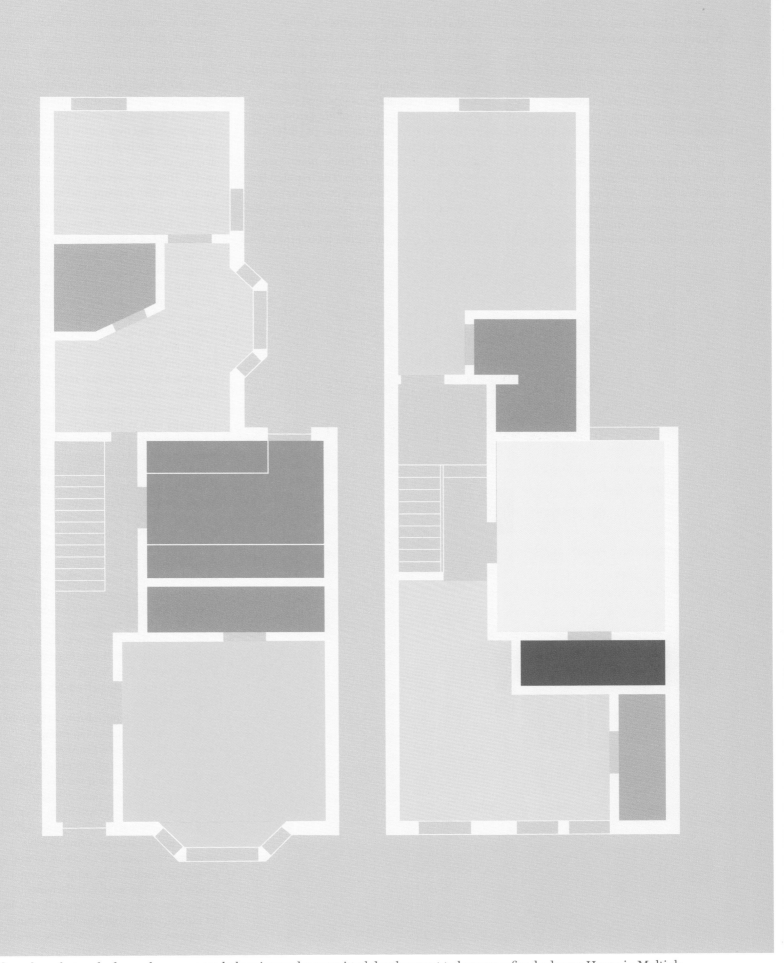

The floorplan of a two-bedroom house granted planning under permitted development to become a five-bedroom House in Multiple Occupancy with shared kitchen

Alan had lived in his sixties townhouse in Lewisham, south-east London, for over 30 years. When he decided to move into a care home, his daughter helped him get the house on to the market.

So far, so ordinary. The family communicated with the buyer who assured them in writing that he wanted to refurbish the property and rent it out as a family home. The sale eventually went through – various types of brinksmanship resulting in a reduction of £40,000 from the original agreement for a cash purchase – and the builders moved in, transforming the house into small single-room bedsits where five households would now share a toilet, bathroom and kitchen. No Portaloo was installed during the extensive works so the builders urinated in the garden until another neighbour complained, at which point tradesmen regularly disappeared into what had until recently been Alan's garden shed.

The property had become an HMO – a House in Multiple Occupancy – as have increasing numbers of family homes across the UK over recent years. The borough has a stock of large Victorian homes that are ripe for developers, says councillor Paul Bell, cabinet member for housing and planning. "They can generate quite a lot of profit. If six people are renting a room, for let's say £600 a month, that's £3,600. The same house you could rent to a family for probably £1,200. That's the extent of the problem."

In 2018, the UK government estimated that there were around 4.5 million people in England housed in around 497,000 HMOs (Lewisham had over 1,000 HMOs registered in the borough in December 2021 with an average of five-to-six households living in each). They have become an important part of English housing and many of them are well run. HMOs soak up need that has evolved for a variety of reasons, for example, the removal of social housing under Right to Buy (councils were not allowed to invest receipts from sales directly back into housing) or the broader housing crisis. New HMOs, however, are increasingly resembling gloomy backpacker hostels rather than flatshares, despite the images that populate property developer blogs showcasing the high yields available to developers looking to extract the exceptional returns offered by this type of accommodation.

Moreover, organisations dealing primarily with vulnerable people – women escaping domestic violence, returning citizens or the previously homeless, for example – can badge their multiple-occupancy housing as "exempt accommodation". This allows landlords access to higher levels of housing benefit if they're offering "more than minimal care, support or supervision", with a near-complete lack of regulatory oversight. It's something that academic Thea Raisbeck described as an "accountability deficit" in housing charity Commonweal's influential report Exempt From Responsibility? Exempt accommodation was designed as a safety net, but risks becoming a poverty trap and one that redistributes vast sums from the public purse into private pockets, often through HMOs.

Prospect Housing, a former registered provider that specialised in exempt accommodation, used Freedom of Information requests to ascertain that £1 billion had been paid out to exempt accommodation providers in 2020.

"There is certainly cash in the system," says Commonweal chief executive Ashley Horsey, adding that easy profits have attracted institutional investors as well as private individuals and property owners. "Sadly it has also attracted elements of criminality and exploitation. If it is indeed £1 billion, surely that should be enough to support the necessary services, ensure good quality accommodation and housing management and allow a reasonable return to property developers and investors."

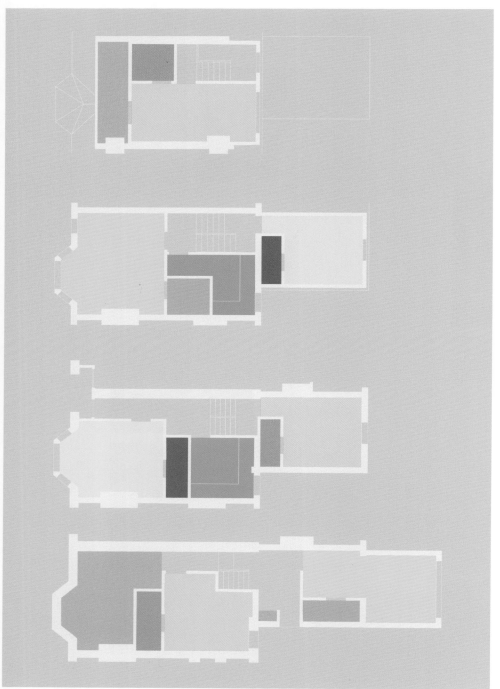

Floorplans in this article are taken from real planning applications for HMOs submitted to city councils across England. The homes typically have shared kitchens, with six to ten bedsits carved out of a two or three-bedroom family home

Accessing some of the £1 billion is relatively easy for anyone with the cash to buy and develop properties like Alan's. An individual or corporate landlord doesn't need permission to turn a family home into an HMO as it's covered by "permitted development" unless there are more than six residents. There is, says Commonweal's policy and communications manager Harry Williams, "astonishing opportunism". He adds that he'd heard of a three-bed family home being turned into 15 units, each of which can be as small as 6.51m². "It's a scandal," he says.

There's certainly a striking difference at work: access to housing benefit has been tightened considerably with the shift to universal credit and the bedroom tax. At the same time it has become extremely easy for wealthy people to suck up huge amounts of benefits through exempt HMOs. It's like the bedroom tax in reverse, where investors can accrue masses of spare rooms, bankrolled by taxpayers.

The lack of regulation stems from exemptions that were made to housing benefit in 1996, removing certain types of accommodation from the usual rent caps. The changes were based on the assumption that participants in this sector would be largely charitable or philanthropic and needed the additional money to support their residents back into stable, mainstream life. Writing in Unherd last November, Niamh Mulvey reported that 150,000 people across the UK are now being housed in exempt accommodation, a 62 per cent increase since 2016. These properties are rarely owned by charities or housing associations; instead they lease them from private landlords or property investors, often through a management company, making accountability even more remote.

This is a national issue, with Birmingham at the sharp end. Whole streets have been

Public funds are being redistributed to private individuals who are protected from regulation or oversight by exempt accommodation loopholes. Many of those newly arrived in the sector are "rogue landlords who are just making as much money as possible"

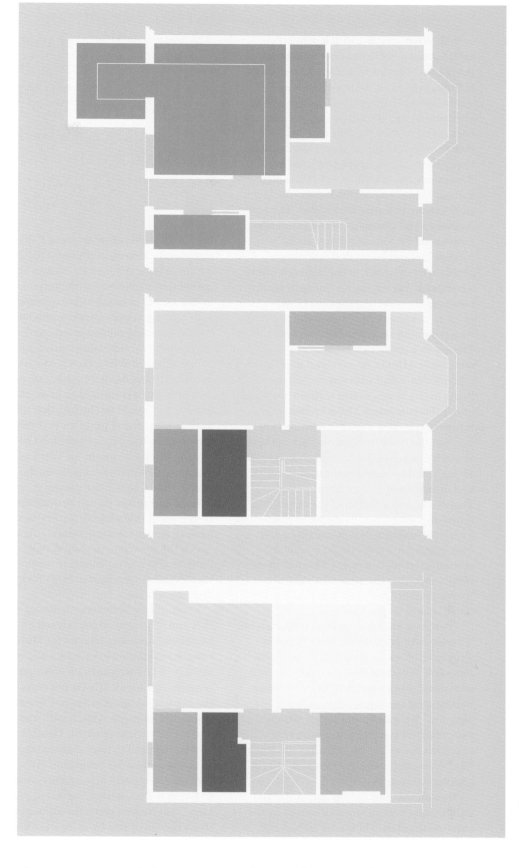

taken over by exempt accommodation HMOs, which were not commissioned by the council and which the council cannot easily regulate. The sector was static between 2016 and 2019 at around 11,000 units, according to Birmingham City Council senior manager of housing strategy Guy Chaundy. By autumn 2021 this had increased to 21,000 units.

The council was one of five areas in the UK awarded over £1.75 million of funding to run a pilot programme aimed at addressing the many problems this type of housing was causing. They've now run 500 inspections with social workers and West Midlands Police, leading to over 200 investigations. The council created various governance and consumer structures alongside a voluntary accreditation scheme, with key referral agencies agreeing to only use accredited properties. The funding also allowed them to improve scrutiny of benefit claims. This particular intervention led to a large number of claims being rejected or stopped, clawing back an estimated £2.5 million, which meant the pilot funding more than paid for itself. They've had a good response from the majority of providers, says Chaundy, and now have "considerable data" on what's being provided and where. The pilot continues and extension funding has been announced for four of the five areas.

Back in Lewisham, Bell describes a problem in the south of the borough where a company was buying up "loads of family homes and converting them to HMOs". He gives an example of a two-bed flat that was converted into six separate households. There's an issue of exploitation of people who live in HMOs, he says, and of residents who suddenly find many more people living in single properties with the practical issues this can bring. These include more refuse or recycling than the existing bins can handle; noise complaints that can't be answered because the council no longer has enough staff to cover non-statutory activity; and occasions of antisocial behaviour. There's also exploitation of the state in terms of public funds being redistributed to private individuals who are protected from regulation or oversight by exempt accommodation loopholes. Many of those newly arrived in the sector, he says, are "rogue landlords who are just making as much money as possible".

It's strong stuff from a local politician but it's even stronger coming from England's Regulator of Social Housing. Deputy chief executive Jonathan Walters outlined the situation during a series of Commonweal webinars on exempt accommodation last autumn. "We have found organisations that were effectively set up as a conduit for others to exploit the rules," he said after the session. "Some housing providers [are] effectively gaming the system."

He said that neither the sector nor the public purse were being well served by the current situation. Things are so bad that the regulator is no longer handing out registered provider status to organisations, in an attempt to cut supply off at the source – although there have been attempts from some landlords to effectively take over existing registered providers as a workaround for some private investors. This is something they are "clamping down on". Commonweal has heard of other workarounds: providers and managing agents of exempt properties shifting away

> "HMOs can generate quite a lot of profit. If six people are renting a room, for let's say £600 a month, that's £3,600. The same house you could rent to a family for probably £1,200. That's the extent of the problem"

from registered provider status to become community interest companies (CICs).

There is an appetite for change at a national level, believes Commonweal's Williams. He cites the select committee of MPs looking at exempt accommodation, the five national pilot schemes, and an opportunity for necessary legislation via the Social Housing White Paper, which came out in 2019 but has yet to generate any new laws. It's a complicated issue, made more complicated by the fact that it's a multidepartmental problem that requires buy-in from the Department for Levelling Up and the Department for Work and Pensions. Commonweal believes the best course would be to offer greater support to local authorities to run accreditation systems and that all local authorities should have an exempt accommodation strategy, which the government should support and fund. It also wants consumer regulation that includes specific standards for exempt accommodation.

Over in Lewisham they're doing what they can. The council introduced an additional licensing scheme for HMOs above commercial premises in 2017 and, from April 2022, will be introducing a new licensing requirement for all HMOs not covered by the existing national scheme. This will set standards for room sizes, health and safety and property management. Landlords will also be required to have clear plans in place to tackle anti-social behaviour. "We plan to visit every property at least once during the five-year licence period," says Bell, "which is a huge undertaking given the amount of money that's been stripped from local government." As well as assessing a new Article 4 Direction which would require HMOs to gain planning permission (but which can be overturned by the secretary of state) they're also consulting on proposals for a new selective licensing scheme covering all privately rented properties in 16 of the borough's 18 wards – although this will also be subject to approval from the secretary of state.

Bell knows the human cost of profit-hungry, unaccountable landlords through casework over nearly 12 years. He also knows it on a personal level, with a family member having to flee domestic violence. "To have those people in an exploited situation, where the landlord doesn't care, is so cruel it's unimaginable," he says. "It shouldn't happen. There are real people on the receiving end of this ... It's appalling."

Emma Warren is an author, editor, journalist and broadcaster with experience in lecturing, workshops and youth work. Her book on the history of a London industrial space and music venue, Make Some Space: Tuning into Total Refreshment Centre, published in 2019, was named one of MOJO magazine's top 10 books of the year

Not least in a pandemic, the World Health Organisation cites several studies that report a direct association between crowded housing and adverse health outcomes, including mental health problems, stress, social tension, sleep disturbances and close-contact infectious diseases

Preview

The Festival of Place 2022
is taking place on 6 July
at Boxpark Wembley, in
Wembley Park, London

The Festival of Place 2022 is moving to Boxpark Wembley, located at the heart of Wembley Park, Quintain's Build-to-Rent neighbourhood, just steps from Wembley Stadium. The inspiring day of talks and workshops will be followed by the awards presentation for The Pineapple awards for place and a good old-fashioned knees-up
Photo: WENN Rights Ltd/Alamy

Festival of Place is back with a one-day event, taking place on 6 July, 2022 at an exciting new venue in the heart of one of Europe's biggest regeneration projects, Boxpark Wembley, in Wembley Park. With over 600 people expected in-person plus a 300-strong digital audience, it's going to be the biggest Festival yet. Tickets are already on sale with a special super early-bird offer, two-for-the price-of-one. Join us for an unmissable day of learning and inspiration.

As ever, the emphasis will be on the spaces between the sessions, through placehacks, workshops, multiple stages, happenings, walking tours and informal networking, ensuring the community can easily make new connections in a relaxed and friendly atmosphere – all to the sound of a mariachi band, with street food and coffee on tap.

Professionals attending will represent private and public sector developers, local and national government, charities and cities, as well as investors, architects, landscape designers, scientists, academics, community outreach workers, activists, artists, and other makers of place. What they share is a common interest in making cities that thrive in the context of large-scale, urban development in the UK.

The event is designed for professionals working in the property sector who want to do things differently. The focus is on the climate and social equity crises as well as how our infrastructure and housing design need to adapt to build better, more inclusive communities. There will be walking tours and interactive seminars that will enliven your professional practice and enhance your creativity, ranging from designing healthy and equitable housing at density to revitalising town centres and developing resilient communities in the midst of a climate emergency.

The idea of a festival is that everyone is free to move around, watching 15 minutes

Wembley and the Olympic Steps during UEFA Euro 2020. Photo: Chris Winter

of one act before going to see another. Participants have the freedom to shape their day and tailor their experience.

Many seminars will be aired live online and made available for on-demand viewing thereafter. So even if you spend all day networking or at the fringe events, you won't miss a thing.

For the first time, The Festival of Place will take place in Boxpark Wembley, located in the heart of Wembley Park, just a stone's throw from Wembley Stadium. Boxpark Wembley hosts an incredibly diverse selection of food traders with a fun selection of leisure activities to enliven the festival atmosphere. It is a unique and versatile event space that will enable the festival to thrive.

We'll also be exploring the 34-hectare Wembley Park, one of Europe's largest regeneration projects. We will be hosting walking tours that look at public realm, buildings, the masterplan, culture, sports and leisure. Quintain is the award-winning development and asset management team behind the scheme.

Last year's Festival of Place in October included walking tours and provocative topics of discussion. Julie Futcher, a lecturer at Anglia Ruskin University, led a walking tour which looked at how a high-rise tower can create a microclimate, even bringing in fresh air and blowing pollution away. She stressed the importance of planning to be geographic, and how building tall or short in the right places can change the weather.

Leonora Grcheva from Doughnut Economics Action Lab, an urban planner, researcher and participation practitioner, demonstrated at the festival how we "unroll the doughnut", showing how the inside contains all the people who are falling short of resources, and the outside represents the planetary boundaries that we must not overstep. Her presentation made an impact on attendee Ellie Cosgrave, a director at urban design and public realm practice at Publica. "Hearing Leonora demonstrating how we can 'unroll the doughnut' in London revealed how we might think about it practically in urban development processes," she said. "Nice!"

Another attendee, Chris Brown, executive and founder of Igloo Regeneration, was particularly interested by a presentation by Loretta Lees, an urbanist and academic who focuses on gentrification, urban public space and architecture. Her talk led him to remark: "If we aren't measuring social capital, social cohesion and wellbeing, we don't understand the damage we are doing. At least 135,000 people have been displaced by council estate gentrification in London."

Other speakers presenting at the Festival

of Place 2021 included: Roger Wade, founder and chief executive of Boxpark; Pooja Agrawal, co-founder and chief executive of Public Practice; architect and developer Martin Prince-Parrot; and Malcolm Hamilton, creative director of Play:Disrupt.

Tim Gill, best selling author of *Urban Playground: How Child-Friendly Planning and Design Can Save Cities* led a morning workshop exploring risk and play in a dynamic way. Patel Taylor ran a walking tour of nearby mixed-use development London Dock. Civic Engineers ran a sketch-like-a-designer workshop exploring the future of high streets and town centres. Participants were also able to explore the concept of the pleasure garden at a workshop with the National Trust's Pam Smith and Vestre's Romy Rawlings which challenged participants to design a contemporary walkable pleasure garden.

Other topics discussed last year included What's the alternative to gentrification? How do we renew places with equity in a climate emergency? Targeting net zero and Why inequality matters – all led by expert and thought-provoking speakers.

Speakers of previous years have included leading developers such as Dan Labbad, then of Lendlease, and Stuart Lipton, partner at Lipton Rogers Developments; scientists and researchers such as Araceli Camargo from Centric Lab and Chanuki Illushka Seresinhe from The Alan Turing Institute; city-shapers such as Tim Tompkins, president of the Times Square Alliance; leading designers such as Bob Allies of Allies and Morrison, Dinah Bornat of ZCD Architects, and Cannon Ivers of LDA Design; and a range of culture, community outreach and arts specialists.

The Placehack workshops presented at the Festival of Place were designed to speak creativity. Participants could get their hands dirty and network while learning new skills and enjoying the moment. In 2019, attendees had the opportunity to work with Andre Reid, founder of Kiondo, to build small-scale models of cities out of salvaged and scrap material; reimagine cities for young families with Urban95; explore authenticity and place branding with Joy Nazzari, founder of dn&co; and experiment with the shape of public spaces to affect behaviour with Nick Tyler, Chadwick chair of civil engineering at UCL.

In 2019, anthropologist Nitasha Kapoor went to the festival to learn what sort of visitors the Festival of Place attracted and how they interacted on the day. She thought it was important to note what attracted people to take a day out of work to be there, and how this type of gathering could help solve pressing problems. "There was a level

Quintain will be leading walking tours of Wembley Park during the Festival to explore the public realm and retail strategy and the unique features of this Build-to-Rent project. Photo: Chris Winter

of joy and fun in the programming that increased the chances of learning something or meeting someone new," she said. "Several people told me that they were there to witness and be a part of something that was different from the start.

"At the Festival of Place, I saw guides everywhere. They were the hosts of the day, chairing panels, leading workshops, standing in the wings, introducing and greeting, actively listening, and connecting people and ideas. They were the shapeshifters who translated presentations into possibilities for creativity. The Festival of Place was ambitious, and it happened. Hundreds of people were there and according to the post-event online survey, two-thirds say they are likely or extremely likely to attend again, with just one person saying they were unlikely to come back.

"What I learned during the live place test was that we have strong and mighty guides among the makers of place, and they play a critical role as informed hosts, gathering different types of people together, making sure everyone feels like they are getting what they need, and challenging us to do better."

Some interesting tweets were posted during last year's event. "Ownership shatters ecology. For the land to survive, for us

to survive, it must cease to be property," Levins Morales tweeted, while Doughnut Economics' Grcheva tweeted about "meeting the needs of all people without breaching the environmental ceiling".

This year's event will be broadcast via the Airmeet platform, which has been serving the festival community through its event-wide chat, popular emoji button, ability to ask questions "on stage," and social lounge featuring video networking tables.

Organisation passes are also available, giving your whole team access to all Festival events, including two tickets to the in-person happening on 6 July.

We believe in inclusivity, which is why we have made sure that, of last year's 46 speakers, 48 per cent were women and 17 per cent were BAME.

Following the festival there will be a celebration at the end of the day of The Pineapple awards for place. Finalists of The Pineapples will come together to celebrate and hand out some prizes. There will be music, dancing, food and fun – an awards celebration like no other.

We believe crucial events like these should be inclusive and cost shouldn't be a barrier, which is why we have arranged free tickets to community groups and small charities

who are interested in attending. Festival of Place 2022 is supported by partners Civic Engineers, Quintain and Vestre.

Find out more, visit festivalofplace.co.uk

Why Peter Barber is the go-to architect for social housing in London

He is a left-winger whose buildings are championed by the right. Laura Mark unpicks the work of the architect and five-strong practice redefining the council flat. Photography by John Sturrock

Donnybrook is the project that got Peter Barber noticed, although his later work abandoned its crisp white render in favour of brick

Last year was a bumper year for architect Peter Barber. He turned 60, became a Royal Academician, received an OBE, was recognised for his contribution to the architectural profession by the Architects' Journal, won the 2021 RIBA Neave Brown Award for his housing scheme at McGrath Road and completed one of his largest schemes yet at 95 Peckham Road, also shortlisted for the award.

The accolades come on the back of an upward trajectory that includes selling out the Barbican's concert hall last year as part of the Architecture Foundation's lecture series and a 2018 Design Museum retrospective exhibition of his work. He's also renowned in architecture circles for his jazz piano playing. *The Guardian*'s architecture critic Oliver Wainwright has called Barber "one of the most original architects working today".

The attention testifies to the impact of Barber and his five-strong practice, which is reimagining traditional housing forms and transforming social architecture.

Based in a former printworks in a small Victorian terrace, Peter Barber Architects' King's Cross studio is crammed with models. Its shop-like window faces out on to the street, inviting passers-by to stop and take a peek. There are news clippings, award certificates and other ephemera stuck to the window. It animates the street and speaks to the work of the architect to the general public walking past.

These clay, plaster and blue foam models that line the walls of the tiny ground-floor meeting space are crucial to the practice's work. Every project starts off as a sketch or model. In Barber's quick pencil crayon sketches there is a sense of urgency.

With between five to eight projects on the go each year, it's hard to believe all of it comes out of such a small practice. "We get work done because everyone is so productive," explains Barber.

The team around him is important, and Barber hates that Covid has meant a move to more homeworking. His staff have all been with him for a long time. His

> "We do housing because it is what the land economy requires but I like to think about it as designing the city. It would be nice if we could have more non-residential stuff – workspaces and shops – but the market is for housing"

> Barber's housing has been used on marketing for organisations such as Create Streets. According to Ben Southwood, previously head of housing at Policy Exchange, Barber is "the Modernist that traditionalists like"

attempts to share credit are noticeable on his Instagram posts.

"We are friends," he says. "We go to the pub. If someone has a birthday we go out. It wouldn't be the same if there were 20 people working here. The smallness is a really important part of who we are as a practice."

Barber, who worked for larger practices including Richard Rogers, Jestico + Whiles and Will Alsop before setting up his own firm in 1989, doesn't want to get any bigger. But his time at these larger practices was formative in his architectural development. His early years were full of High-Tech, but he grew to be more interested in buildings that were grounded and solid; the works of Luis Barragan and Álvaro Siza became his inspiration. But it was a project for Jestico + Whiles in the Docklands in the 1980s that got him into housing.

"Unlike a lot of things going up at the time, this was street-based housing, and I really got into that," he says. Barber is now known as the go-to architect for social housing in the capital.

"Although the best shorthand for our work is housing, I like to think of it as urban architecture," he says. "We do housing because it is what the land economy requires but I like to think about it as designing the city, and it would be nice if our projects could have more non-residential stuff in them – workspaces and shops – but the market is for housing."

Barber qualified as an architect in 1985 when the Modernist ideals of sixties mass housing were being rejected and the council estate was portrayed as a place of crime and social breakdown. Thatcher was in the process of disbanding local authority architect departments, forcing the sell-off of council housing stock and preventing the building of any new social housing.

"That era when people were very politicised rubbed off on me a bit," he says with a grin. It's easy to link Thatcher's dismantling of social housing with the trajectory of Barber's work but he says his politicisation came before that.

When he had just finished school, Barber spent a year in South Africa in 1979, working as part of the maintenance and building team for a multiracial school during the apartheid era. That was what "really got me into building", he says, but adds that "it probably got me into politics too". He came back and worked a year in a local architecture practice before heading to Sheffield University to study architecture.

Barber is a vocal and progressive lefty – always has been. It is where politics and housing meet that he is most critical of government systems.

"The realisation of how many empty homes there are, is shocking," he tells me. "There are 160,000 empty homes in the UK and around 160,000 homeless people. There are enough homes to go around. Yes, there are a lot of homes in London used as investment vehicles, but the biggest factor is that homes are empty because areas have become depopulated.

"Then you start to think more about the politics of architecture, and it goes much further than just building homes, to where resources are allocated. If you had a government that believed in a managed economy more, business would be encouraged to go and settle in these areas rather than everything being in London."

He also calls for increased spending on social housing, an end to Right to Buy, and rent controls for private landlords.

Yet, paradoxically, Barber's housing designs have been taken up by the right, who see their low-rise, high-density as appealing to their own traditional narrative. His urban design style has been used on propaganda-like marketing for organisations such as Create Streets and right-leaning thinktank Policy Exchange. According to Ben Southwood, previously head of housing at

The small windows in the seafoam front doors at Donnybrook have been papered over by residents with postcards or fabric

Donnybrook, with its outdoor spaces, oriel windows and private front doors is cited as good design in the government's latest design code

Barber on Donnybrook: "It was a celebration of the public, social life of the street. It was our rallying cry"

The 42 two and three-storey terraces at Donnybrook, built for housing association Circle 33 and shortlisted for the 2006 RIBA Stirling Prize

Signs of life at Donnybrook as photographed in January 2022

The balconies at Donnybrook are in need of renewal. Barber now opts for materials such as brick that require less maintenance

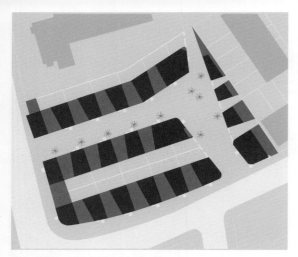

Site plan of Donnybrook

Policy Exchange, Barber is "the Modernist that traditionalists like".

When I ask how he feels about his architecture being used by these organisations, he jokes: "It is worrying. My response is: 'Oh crumbs!'" He says the Create Streets crowd have been in touch, as well as the late Roger Scruton before his death in 2020. "We just have to carry on doing what we think is right. If it has popular appeal, then I don't mind that."

The government's latest design code guidance cites one of Barber's earlier schemes, Donnybrook, as an example of good design. But the scheme wouldn't have gone ahead if it hadn't been for Richard Rogers' Urban Task Force in the nineties, which aimed to tackle some of the issues caused by Thatcherism and Conservative housing policy.

"Richard Rogers' Urban Task Force was a significant factor in this project," says Barber. "We couldn't have done it five years earlier. The Urban Task Force really helped change things."

Donnybrook, the result of a competition held by the Architecture Foundation for housing on a site in Bow, east London, was the project that really launched Barber and got him noticed. It also landed him a spot on the 2006 RIBA Stirling Prize shortlist.

"There are 160,000 empty homes in the UK and around 160,000 homeless people. There are enough homes to go around. Yes, there are homes in London used as investment vehicles, but the biggest factor is that areas have become depopulated"

Seen as creating a new piece of city and stitching itself into the existing streetscape, it consisted of 42 two and three-storey terraces for the housing association Circle 33.

With its individual front doors and private outdoor spaces, it is where we first see the characteristics that now typify Barber's housing design, even if he now uses brick instead of distinctive white-rendered facades.

Barber chooses brick for the simplest of reasons: render doesn't get properly maintained by landlords. Donnybrook has been well looked after but you can still see areas where graffiti has been hastily painted over. And now, 15 years after its completion, its painted balconies are beginning to look tired and in need of attention.

When presenting Donnybrook in lectures, Barber often mentions the small windows in the front doors, which residents have covered up with posters and patterned papers – a clear message that this design gesture did not work. Barber delights in this small act of customisation as a "nice surprise" despite it showing up this apparent design error.

He admits there was a "naivety" about Donnybrook. "Everything was wrong with it as far as standards were concerned," he says. "It didn't fit on the site. At the time it felt like a sensible normal thing to be doing but I look back at it and I think: oh bloody hell!"

He adds: "It was a celebration of the public, social life of the street. It was our rallying cry. And it is what now comes out over and over again in our projects."

The practice's subsequent schemes have featured influences from Borromini to Le Corbusier and Louis Kahn. But they all explore the traditional English housing type, whether it be terraces, back-to-backs, courtyard blocks or almshouses.

Although most of his schemes are apartments, they have the feeling of houses. It's about the front door. He harks back to designs for cottage flats, which each had a front door to the street.

Most of his projects sit on small plots of leftover land thought by others to be undevelopable. Both Bevan Road in Abbey Wood, for Greenwich Council, and Hannibal Road Gardens in Stepney for Southern Housing Group were squeezed on to sites previously occupied by garages; another scheme near Portobello Road, which he is currently working on, will occupy a narrow embankment of the Circle Line.

Many of Barber's motifs are repeated throughout his projects. Brick arches which act as thresholds to the street, a kind of English stoop, are seen at McGrath Road, Bevan Road and Ordnance Road. Oriel-style corner windows can be seen at Donnybrook, 95 Peckham Road and Bevan Road. The

wavy roofline of Ilchester Road, his housing scheme for older residents in Barking, is repeated again at Holmes Road, Camden, a housing scheme for homeless people.

He admits to not starting every project from scratch. "It's what makes us efficient," he says. "We know what works; we've tried and tested it. Each design is iterative. There are themes – about the street, and unusual typologies. We don't have to invent everything from first principles each time."

The floorplan of the ground-floor two-bedroom flats at Donnybrook, with two-bedroom maisonette above

Barber learns from how residents have adopted and customised elements of his projects

A drawing of the gardens at Holmes Road, Camden, studio accommodation for single homeless people with support needs, completed in 2016

100 Mile City is a concept for suburbia that unlocks land: a linear city that's 100 miles long, 200 metres wide and four storeys high

Inside a studio flat at Holmes Road, Camden in 2016. Photo: Morley von Sternberg

McGrath Road includes 26 homes in "tower houses", each set over three or four storeys, in a back-to-back layout with private front door, balcony, terrace, a top-floor living room with views and a shared courtyard

Site plan of the back-to-back homes at McGrath Road. Barber often revisits traditional English housing types

Through the arch and into the communal courtyard. A two-bedroom freehold "tower house" is listed on Purple Bricks for £500,000

Barber says private doors to the street precludes the need for 'poor doors' or distinct entrances for each tenure

The internal courtyard of McGrath Road is a communal space gated to the street. Photo: Morley von Sternberg

The celebration of the street remains a focus of Barber's work, with the brick arch used to mark a threshold between public and private space

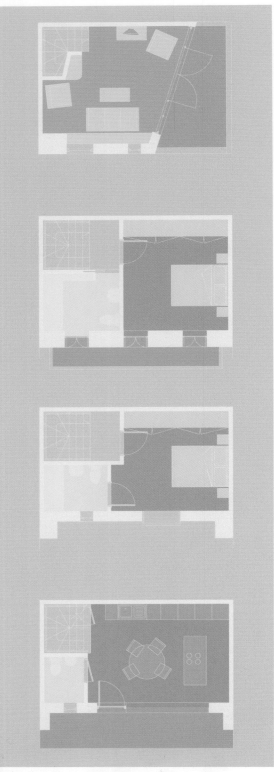

A typical floorplan at McGrath Road with a ground floor kitchen, top-floor living room, two bedrooms and three bathrooms

Although brick has now become synonymous with his design aesthetic, Barber does question its use. "One of the disappointments for me is that brick and concrete are not ecological materials. But unfortunately, we are lumbered with them because of the mayor's directive on building materials."

Barber is working on a demonstration housing scheme in the German city of Fulda where he's using timber for both the structure

"In Fulda in Germany, they have got it right. They are building a park, a beer hall, an ice rink, a zoo, and when all that is done, all the infrastructure is in place, then they will do our housing scheme"

and the external envelope. "They are wanting an exhibition piece of housing," he says. "They have got it right. They are building a park, a beer hall, an ice rink, a zoo, and when all that is done, all the infrastructure is in place, then they will do our housing scheme." The 90-home scheme will be an interesting move for the practice and a test of whether their ideas translate out of the London vernacular.

Back in London, their next project to complete bounds the North Circular Road in Finchley on a site owned by Transport for London. Part of the GLA Small Sites Programme, the development will protect existing houses from the six-lane motorway while creating around 100 new homes. It's reminiscent of Neave Brown's Alexandra Road but with the concrete replaced by brick and some Barber details thrown in too. Barber jokes that it's just short of the length of Alexandra Road. For the practice, it's a move away from a local authority client and onto a much bigger plot of land, although not without difficulties and constraints. An architect I spoke to about the project commented that he couldn't believe someone was finally building on that land. "The client [Kuropatwa] is fearless," says Barber. "It is a private developer and they will take calculated risks in the way that a local authority client won't."

Speaking about the project, he adds: "Things do move along. There are recognisable themes there but there is also a lot going on in that project which we've never done before."

Barber's work is about a reinvention of the traditional housing-type and this is blended with his own political voice that shapes the architecture and shows a care for the people who will walk his streets and inhabit his buildings. But it's not all rosy. Barber himself is critical of the way his work is used and idealised. "There are more than 6,000 homeless people in London. There are just 40 to 50 rooms at our Holmes Road project. It isn't really doing very much. It is a Band-Aid. Doing a high-profile project like that is diverting our attention from the real problem."

And for that reason, Barber says he would like to get even deeper into politics. "I'd like to speak to the housing secretary or someone about policy. Sorting out VAT on refurbishment, diversion of resources away from London to other areas with empty buildings," Barber concludes. "There is a long list of things which are peripheral, but all connected to architecture."

Laura Mark is a film-maker, architecture critic, editor and curator. She is the Keeper at Walmer Yard, a set of four houses in Notting Hill designed by Peter Salter. Mark is co-leader for first year at Sheffield School of Architecture and is undertaking a PhD at Newcastle University exploring our experience of the home.

Beechwood Mews, Barnet, includes 97 homes (50 per cent affordable) arranged along a pedestrianised street, with a cafe and corner shop

Placetest: Nine Elms

What is the experience of this nascent place and its people? Anthropologist Caroline Bennett visits Nine Elms and speaks to locals and residents with photography by John Sturrock

In 2013, Arthur Kay published a short story called Paranoia House. Set in 2062, it describes how Terrence Fyed lives in a constant state of fear and paranoia; of violence, terrorism, and climate emergency. He has adapted his house to protect himself, his fears heightened by direct threats in the area in which he lives – close to the Thames, close to Battersea Power Station, close to the US Embassy. He lives in Nine Elms.

That a dystopian story should be set in the South London neighbourhood says interesting things about the imagination of the area. In many ways, Nine Elms fits a dark futuristic aesthetic – tall and hard-surfaced, with little green and, as of yet, a limited population. Walking around, you are struck by concrete, steel, glass. Everything is high rise. Design elements aiming to emphasise luxury abound: waterfalls near the US Embassy; a sunken garden; glass-fronted restaurants that span whole sides of buildings. There is a static cycling studio, a salon, an Instagrammable cafe filled with flowers and, of course, the infamous Sky Pool – a private transparent swimming pool that floats between two towers.

Everywhere is building work. Cranes litter the skyline. The roads are busy from morning to night with trucks bringing materials or taking rubble away. Tubes pump concrete up to floors in the sky. Large areas are blocked off from public access, surrounded by hoardings advertising the future to come, some with art. The air is full of dust. It's noisy all the time. But in this construction zone is life. The area is teaming with communities although perhaps not those you might expect.

As one of the last major post-industrial zones to be redeveloped in the capital, the Vauxhall Nine Elms Battersea Opportunity Area planning framework was published in 2012 with a forward by London's then mayor Boris Johnson.

At 227 hectares (561 acres), Nine Elms is the largest regeneration project in London (some claim in Europe), and the plans are staggering in ambition: more than 42 building projects; 20,000 new homes bringing an estimated 30,000 new residents to the area; 25,000 new jobs after construction; 22,000 during; a new town centre; two new tube stations; and a new bridge across the Thames.

The Nine Elms Vauxhall Partnership, led by Wandsworth and Lambeth Councils, includes all the big names, from developers such as Berkeley Group, Barratt, Taylor Wimpey, Ballymore, St Modwen, and Mount Anvil, to architects including Frank Gehry, Zaha Hadid Architects and Foster + Partners, representing billions of pounds of investment.

In any living space there is a common area for bringing people together. In villages, there's the village green, around which would sit a pub, a church and the village shop. In urban areas, there are squares. As of yet, Nine Elms has no such space. I was wandering about, thinking, "Where would the buskers go?"

Much has been written about the area, with a focus on its extravagance, the international investor funding model, its lack of character and the perceived social segregation – the so-called "spatial apartheid" where facilities and entrances are restricted to certain residents.

Writing for *The Guardian*, Oliver Wainwright says of Nine Elms: "If it is an opportunity area, it has been an opportunity for trialling a new form of social apartheid on an industrial scale."

Edwin Heathcote, architecture critic for the *Financial Times*, describes Nine Elms as the "privatisation of formerly public lands to create an ad-hoc pile-up of towers" and "a massive missed opportunity for a serious piece of city on a remarkable site".

Spending time in the area reveals other stories, however; important stories that tell of the wider community and the lives entwined and affected by the Nine Elms development.

These are stories of rhythm and space, flows of traffic, disconnection and exclusion, but also of communities of belonging, widened opportunities, shrinking spaces bringing people closer together, and layers of the past that push through the futuristic architecture to stubbornly complicate new stories told so far.

The interviews take place in Nine Elms in the final months of 2021. Some names have been changed to protect anonymity.

Life in Nine Elms
Frankie moved to the area in 2020 into housing provided by her employer. While she works for them, she remains living there. "This is a construction zone," she says. "I live in a construction zone."

For Frankie, the height of the buildings and their proximity to one another makes establishing community difficult. The towers block out the light, there is too much concrete. "There's nothing homey or comfortable or aesthetically pleasing about this area," she comments.

Frankie uses the supermarkets – Waitrose in New Union Square, and Sainsbury's now that a cut-through to Wandsworth Road has opened up. But for social events, or just finding spaces to relax, she leaves Nine Elms, heading towards Battersea or further out. "That's where the community places are," she notes. "[Nine Elms] is just construction. There's nothing. I can't think of anything that's over there. It's just something in between Battersea and Vauxhall itself … It's a place that you go through. It's not a place that you go to."

Frankie's house is one of the new blocks at Nine Elms, close to Battersea. There are things she loves about the area: the park, the Uber Boat, the fact that she can walk to work if she wants to. But overall, it's not an area she would choose. "This isn't what I think of when I think about London," she comments. "I wanted something, I don't know, Victorian, I guess. This is so modern. It doesn't feel like I'm in London. It feels like I could be in any city. It's basically soulless."

The "soullessness" of Nine Elms is noted by others, but what it means varies. For the people I speak to, it relates to community as much as design. Although the high-rises feel generic and the restaurants have the look of a thousand others, the crux of it is what this aesthetic engenders: the inability to be a local. As Frankie notes: "I think part of having a community is feeling like, 'Oh, this is our spot. Yeah. This is our pub. This is our cafe.' There's nothing like that around here to set your mark on."

Mila moved to Nine Elms in 2017, only moving out last year when the opening of the Sky Pool and the two new tube stations increased her rent to a level she could no longer afford. In general, Mila feels very positive about Nine Elms. As someone with an underlying health condition and busy with postgraduate study, being somewhere with all the amenities on tap is attractive. She was looking for a new-build with its related benefits for accessibility. She was also drawn to the location: "There's a certain cachet to living in Nine Elms," she notes. According to Zoopla, the average sold price for a property in the area is £675,483.

Like Frankie, Mila notes a lack of community. "There are a lot of empty units, sadly; people who are not living there full-time. And that makes it hard to know your neighbours and have that community atmosphere." There are places to go, Mila says, but as a local you aren't guaranteed to get in. Bars and restaurants stretch along

The US Embassy, top right, is the most secure ever built. Its blast zone, defensive landscaping and high-tech surveillance dominate Nine Elms

The new tube stations are a draw, but have also led to an increase in the cost of rent for some

The Vauxhall Nine Elms Battersea Opportunity Area includes Battersea Power Station and New Covent Garden Market. Drawing: SOM

the riverside from Vauxhall through Nine Elms all the way to the power station. It's a new hub for London, but if you live in the area, it's hard to find space. "It's just a bit frustrating," Mila comments. "When you live there and you can't get a table … especially after Covid. Part of what you want to do when you live in an area is go: 'I've got my local restaurant that I really like. A cafe that I go to.'" Mila went down to the pub when the Euros were on, but because she hadn't booked, there was no space, and nowhere to go nearby. "That's not what a local should be like," she says.

The lack of social space isn't only a problem for residents. Everyone mentions it. There's an assumption that it's the nature of the buildings that makes it hard to create community, not only because so many units remain empty, but because they are high rather than wide. "This is one of the very few areas that is almost exclusively, if not completely, high or medium rise," says Betsy Blatchley, a reverend who works in the area and lives close by. "There are virtually no houses in Nine Elms. And that has an impact."

In 2018, the Diocese of Southwark appointed Blatchley as pioneer minister in the arts for the Church of England, leading the Nine Elms Art Ministry. Seeing the plans for development in the area, the diocese saw the arts as a route to connect with the growing population. She finds the area and her work exciting but the nature of Nine Elms has made it challenging.

Although Nine Elms is not a gated community, there are elements of restriction. Its vertical nature means people don't connect with one another in the same way as inhabitants with front doors do. Many of the developments also come with associated services: their own gym, pool, concierge, laundry and garden. People don't need to

> The lack of social space isn't only a problem for residents. Everyone mentions it. There's an assumption that it's the nature of the buildings that makes it hard to create community, not only because so many units remain empty, but because they are high rather than wide

The US Embassy lies at the heart of the plan. Drawing: SOM

leave their building and, even when they do, places to come together are limited.

The commons
In any living space there is a common area for bringing people together. In traditional villages, there's the village green, around which would sit a pub, a church and the village shop. In urban areas, there are city squares.

With Nine Elms Park due to complete in 2025, as of yet, Nine Elms has no such space. New Union Square has the name of one but it's actually a pedestrianised pathway connecting Nine Elms Lane and Malthouse Road. I noticed the lack of a common when I was wandering about, thinking: "Where would the buskers go? Where would you put on plays? Play music? Dance?"

Astrid, who lives nearby, comments: "There's nowhere to sit and stay. Well, there is, but only if you're buying something. But there's nowhere to sit and have a natter. And where would I take my child?"

At the heart of Nine Elms is the US Embassy, the most secure building in Britain, with its crescent moat, bomb-blast zone, Faraday cage and high-tech surveillance.

Like many other developments, all the spaces that appear to be public are in fact privately owned, and while they may be accessible to the public, their owners can impose restrictions on access and use, for example limiting photographs, moving people on, or banning protest, making them less than public in reality. At Nine Elms, Wandsworth is said to be enacting London's first charter for privately owned public space to secure the space for leisure and wellbeing.

What counts as Nine Elms varies depending on who you ask and where you look. The Vauxhall Nine Elms Battersea Opportunity Area spans from Vauxhall Bridge all the way down to Battersea Park, encompassing the power station and surrounding areas. This is the development

area as identified in the original 2004 London Plan, which transformed the approach of London development. Instead of focusing on boroughs and their related centres (Brixton and Wandsworth), it identified underdeveloped and neglected brownfield sites on the peripheries: King's Cross in the north, Liverpool Street to the east, Nine Elms in the west.

In contrast, what Wandsworth and Lambeth call "Nine Elms on the South Bank" stretches all the way from Lambeth Palace to Battersea Park, and southwards to include Lambeth College on Wandsworth Road. This is an aspirational area that encompasses cultural and community policies as well as the wider building work.

The district of Nine Elms itself denotes the area around the new US Embassy, from Vauxhall Cross down Nine Elms Lane to just south of New Covent Garden Market. The different names and geographies reflect the dizzying array of organisations, plans and strategies involved in the redevelopment – a collaborative affair between the Greater London Authority, Lambeth and Wandsworth Councils, the London Development Agency, Transport for London and English Heritage. The development's implementation involves yet further parties: 42 different developers, many of whom work with multiple partners and contract out aspects of work, leaving the final count almost impossible to quantify. Each of these comes with its own idea of where and what Nine Elms is, and a development plan related to this.

With so many different investors, developers, businesses and buildings, it is hard to create the kind of connections that make community. In this regard, Blatchley is someone who can make such connections. She works across the development with the councils, developers, local schools, community groups and individuals. Although she is a minister, she says her role is to connect people – "to make ways for people to encounter one another, and to create community through that." The church is doing this through the arts.

It's been standard practice to involve the cultural industries in urban redevelopment – for the optimistic, as a way to bring meaning, depth and culture to an area; for cynics, as a way to paper over issues of discomfort, disingenuities and disappointments. At Nine Elms, key stakeholders from government, developers and the Church of England have seen the arts as a means to connect with the community, made visible in large-scale commissioned spaces, such as the Thames Walk pavilion by architects Studio Weave

Modern Marriage (2014) by artist Simon Fujiwara in Embassy Gardens. A public art trail runs from Battersea Park to Vauxhall through Nine Elms

with print artist Linda Florence, to art on hoardings and cladding around the area.

Art has provided a significant opportunity to draw people into Nine Elms. Throughout December, the Nine Elms Advent Calendar Art Trail (organised by Nine Elms Art Ministry) displayed 24 installations across the redevelopment zone in an attempt to connect new and established communities. The Line of Light festival, mapping the route of the new Northern Line extension, brought people from Oval via Stockwell past Nine Elms tube station to the power station.

The council is encouraging cultural anchor tenants to connect with areas neglected by the development, such as the Patmore Estate and local schools. The newly opened Merchants Way ("the cut-through", as everyone calls it) has helped with this. Wide, open and sided by colourful boarding, with a rainbow crossing connecting to Arch 42, it creates a route under the railway lines, more than halving the time between Wandsworth Road and Nine Elms Lane, bringing these two communities closer together. But there remains a disconnection between old and new.

From the outskirts, this disconnect looks problematic. But as with every place, there are a multitude of realities and ways of looking. Nine Elms is a story of redevelopment and gentrification – but not the same old story. This is not Elephant and Castle, where existing homes were destroyed to make way for new estates, displacing communities and creating demographic change through development. Nine Elms was a post-industrial brownfield site; nobody was decanted or relocated.

Some locals express concern about development creep. Lambeth College on Wandsworth Road is inside the development zone and there are plans to build a 27-storey student residence next to the existing college. It will overshadow three Victorian terraces that remain in the area, blocking their sunlight. There's also been an increase in flooding to the area. Laura says: "The Victorian drains are bursting. Maybe they'd burst anyway, but is the development making it happen more often?"

World leading
There's something aspirational to Nine Elms. It's an area of firsts and mosts. The biggest redevelopment zone in London. The world's first swimming pool bridge. The longest roof garden in London. The tallest residential building in Europe. These statements are reminiscent of Dubai, a city created out of a desert, which relied on impressive architecture and world-record claims to attract businesses and tourists. Nine Elms

There is a wealth divide between Nine Elms and the surrounding areas as well as within the developments themselves, although accusations of social apartheid are frankly ridiculous. Weaponising a term of violence by using it to describe access to gym memberships and a swimming pool is insulting. That said, aspects of the wealth gap in the area can feel obscene

is trying to make a global splash, and there's something exciting about that.

Laura and Pat, Astrid, Ursula, Liam and Matt all live in a community close to the new Nine Elms tube station. Each of them owns their place, bought because they want to build a home. They all commented favourably on the transport links and facilities available. The new Underground station was part of the draw for Laura, Pat, Liam and Matt in coming to the area. Ironically, Trump refused to visit the new US Embassy on his visit in 2018 because of its "lousy location" – a fact that for some in the area is a point of pride.

For Ursula, who moved here in 1986, the tube is a bonus, but also irrelevant. Now that the cut-through link has opened between Wandsworth Road and Nine Elms Lane, she is enjoying the changes. "I love the way that they're trying to connect this side with that side," she says. "It's great that you can walk from here and get to another coffee shop in 10 minutes – to District (I love it!), to a posh supermarket." They enjoy the buzz of the new restaurants and cafes, and connections to the river. They feel Transport for London's redesignation of the area to Zone 1 adds status to their homes.

The overall development plan references placemaking as a key part of the restructure with mixed communities of living: residences, shops, leisure facilities and space. But the full development, including many of the key aspects aimed at creating community are not yet in place. The linear park, the community hub, the new school, cinema and theatre, and the services needed to support community living like doctors and dentists and garden centres, for example, aren't expected to finish

until 2025. That it has not yet created a sense of community might be down to design but it could also be a function of time and construction phasing. Places are created by people and their movement and relationship with space. According to geographer Doreen Massey, they are formed through an ongoing negotiation between space, community, politics, history, economies, and time. They cannot be designed, because they are organic, and attempts to overmanage community can create barriers to belonging.

The wealth gap
There is a wealth divide between Nine Elms and the surrounding areas as well as within the developments themselves, although accusations of social apartheid are frankly ridiculous. Weaponising a term of violence by using it to describe access to gym memberships and a swimming pool is insulting. That said, aspects of the wealth gap in the area can feel obscene.

Arriving at Nine Elms to conduct interviews, I came via a food bank in Vauxhall where I volunteer. Every week it feeds between 30 and 40 families, relying on donated food from local shops and people, much of which is past its best. This is only one of scores of food banks in the area – small scale, run by religious organisations of all types, not recorded by the government, yet depended upon by many in the local community. As I moved from one space to the other, the difference was stark. Our shabby food bank is messy and vibrant, full of life, chatter and normalcy. As I crossed the Wandsworth Road and made my way to the cut-through, the surroundings began to change. Colour and disorganisation faded into browns and straight lines. As I walked into the cafe where I was to meet the manager, the concierge greeted me by calling me ma'am, the most generic of all terms. The coffee cost almost £5.

Exclusion doesn't only happen through forced relocation. As other academics studying urban redevelopment have pointed out, it can happen through spatial design and rhythmic restructuring. The Nine Elms architecture is built in such a way as to disguise deprivation in the area and keep it away. The housing shelter that used to be at Vauxhall bus station has been shifted backward out of view. While the power station has a few areas to rest, the only areas to sit in Nine Elms are big concrete blocks outside the US Embassy – too far apart to encourage conversation, overlooked by high rises and glass-fronted bars. Some see these aspects as positive. To Archie, who moved jobs from Soho to Nine Elms to manage the restaurant at Linnaean (he has since

Florian (2013), a giant cast marrow in polished bronze by Sarah Lucas in Embassy Gardens

left), they are signifiers of safety: the area is lit, it's clean, there's no space to loiter or hide. Ironically, according to the Mayor of London's crime map, the area has higher crime rates than neighbouring wards in Wandsworth, and the most recent numbers show crime is rising.

What makes this area feel safe and attractive for some is exclusionary to others. If the weather is bad, there's nowhere to go except into a place where you have to buy something. When the builders break for lunch, they go to the riverside where there are wooden benches, open sky, and a more welcoming feel. If you are a rough sleeper, the only place to find shelter is the Nine Elms Pavilion on the riverside, opened in 2018. Though, as Liam points out, the problem isn't the developers, or the businesses per se. They are profit-driven enterprises. The issue is the government policy to privatise public space.

Mila says she moved out not only because of the rent increase but because she felt the price points at Nine Elms attract people with lifestyles not commensurate with everyday life: parties at all times; loud roaring cars at all hours of the night; cafes that open at 8 or 9am, and close at 3pm. There's no place for shift workers to grab coffee or lunch at a non-standard hour. It may suit certain lives, but it forces others to find lives elsewhere.

Rhythms and communities of belonging
If you stop and listen, Nine Elms is teaming with life. From 7am, a stream of construction workers emerge from Vauxhall Station, stopping at Tesco, grabbing coffee from Pret. They arrive from all over London, and many originally from elsewhere. A queue starts to form outside the US Embassy around 7:15. Just before eight, parents start moving through with children – pushing buggies, or with kids on scooters and bikes. By 8:30, District – the most approachable coffee shop – is filled with people, some sitting in, though mostly grabbing takeaway coffees and pastries on their way to work. Then come the dog-walkers and the runners, taking advantage of the river walkway and the spaces between the buildings, linking Lambeth and Wandsworth Road to the river. Throughout the day, the area is covered in noise, dirt, movement and laughter. The flow reverses around six o'clock, depending on the day, as workers go back home.

Communities of belonging are beginning to emerge. With Covid, many businesses that had planned to open were delayed or closed, with a few having found new ways of offering services. Places have started to open up again now but, being a brand new area in a post-lockdown era, forecasting was hard. Some businesses got it wrong. Covid

brought them together to help each other. When an establishment's ice machine broke down, another business gave them ice. There are several WhatsApp groups for residents. When Mila was shielding, her neighbours took her bins out, got her shopping and looked out for her.

The disconnection between Nine Elms and its surrounding communities is also changing. As Ursula put it, the area is shrinking, and with that comes integration. "Integration is something that's interesting to think about," she says. "I think it's something that's going to take time. But I think that [will happen] the more the demographic changes, as the demographic gets younger."

Nine Elms has a long and varied past, but has always been a place of new ventures as well as contrasts. In 1760, the artist Samuel Scott, a contemporary of Hogarth, painted the original Nine Elms and the slums behind it, as viewed from across the river in Pimlico. Along with the slums were gas works, candle makers, and other industries. In the 19th century, Charlotte Despard, a wealthy campaigning socialite for adults and then women's suffrage, chose Nine Elms as her battleground, moving there in the 1890s. The cabinet's first working class MP, John Burns, was born in Vauxhall. The first station for the London and South Western Railway was at Nine Elms. After it finished transporting passengers, more than 800 steam locomotives were built by the railway at Nine Elms.

In the latter half of the 20th century, the area was all but abandoned. The first phase of the power station, Battersea A, opened in 1935, it was Grade II listed in 1980, and decommissioned in 1983. The cold store at the top of the road, built in 1964 on land previously used by the South Metropolitan Gas Works (which had itself been built on the site of a former tidal mill), was disused from 1979 and demolished in 1999. For years, Nine Elms was a post-industrial wasteland, inaccessible to most. It took a long time for the new development to get off the ground, but it's now well underway.

Walking around Nine Elms, it feels a little Haussmannian; everything razed to the ground to begin again. But if you look closely, elements of the past jut into the present; pieces of history that refuse to be erased. Along the river's edge are Riverside and Elm Quay Courts – red brick developments from the 1980s that break up the skyline of the new-builds surrounding them. There's Tideway Village, a collection of houseboats which fought to remain. The terracotta relief River God (Father Thames), constructed in 1988, refers to the millennia that people have been worshipping the Thames, often in the

The popular District coffee shop

very area now being redeveloped. There's Battersea Power Station itself, an icon, a megastructure, a monument, now corralled by new developments to the south.

When the Thames recedes, mudlarkers come and collect what they find – glass bottles and old clay pipes. You can see remnants of places that came before – a stratigraphy of the past, all but erased by the present development. Some of these are significant: upstream from Vauxhall Bridge are the remnants of a Bronze Age causeway estimated to be from around 1500BC, and downstream there are six prehistoric timber piles from around 6,000 years ago – London's oldest structure, discovered in 2011 alongside Mesolithic tools and Neolithic pottery. It sits at the confluence of the Thames and the Effra – streams that existed in south London but have since been culverted and used for sewage. Less romantic but equally vital is the Thames Water Heathwall pumping station – an ugly grey building that dominates Nine Elms Lane where it stands.

"There is a resurrection of Nine Elms right now and the area is completely changing," Archie says at the end of our interview. "It's a new history starting." The thing about history is that it's never stagnant and it never completely disappears. In so-called "placemaking", previous pasts are integrated in the present, even in industrial zones and on brownfield sites that seem empty and ripe for new life.

While he looks to the future, the past appeals to Archie too: "There's so much history, I can see that," he says. "These old pipes, the people that were standing next to the piers, smoking a pipe, talking."

Caroline Bennett is associate research fellow in cultural anthropology at the School of Social and Cultural Studies, Te Herenga Waka – Victoria University of Wellington, New Zealand

The 50-storey DAMAC Tower offers luxury apartments, a 23rd floor swimming pool and interiors designed by Donatella Versace

Nine Elms residents accept that, for the time being at least, they live on a construction site, with Nine Elms Park due to complete in 2025

Delays to the One Nine Elms towers are expected due to a late payment from client R&F Properties, one of China's biggest developers

The US Embassy feels like the focal point of the development at this stage, although this could shift as the site is built out

There is a strong Portuguese community, as seen here on Wilcox Road, also home to the laundrette in 1985 film *My Beautiful Laundrette*

The cut-through to Wandsworth Road makes it easier for Nine Elms residents to get to the local Sainsbury's

Residents of the Wyvil Estate just outside Nine Elms have spoken out about rising rents and fears they are being pushed out

The riverside walk in Nine Elms has been commended for opening up access to the Thames for pedestrians

Merchants Way, wide, open and sided by colourful boarding, more than halves the journey between Wandsworth Road and Nine Elms Lane

Text on signage within the image:
← NEW COVENT GARDEN MARKET
← FOOD EXCHANGE
← PONTON ROAD
← RIVER THAMES

A raised garden by Studio Weave references the site's industrial heritage in its use of copper-coated water tank panels. The patterns, designed by print artist Linda Florence, were inspired by colourful bridges built during the industrial revolution

Two swings in Nine Elms across from the US Embassy – currently the only public play equipment in the area until Nine Elms Park is complete

The rainbow crossing from Merchant's Way to the archway leading to the Nine Elms Estate

The Sky Pool has become the flashpoint for debate about spatial segregation on site and the growing wealth gap in the wider area

Black Lives Matter stencilled on the pavement near the US Embassy at Nine Elms

Large areas of Nine Elms are behind hoardings with imagery that reveals the historic and new narratives being promoted by stakeholders

THAMES CITY

SQUARE   HYATT

R&F Property UK's new developments
are located at the heart of the Nine Elms
regeneration area.

Here in the area will altogether comprise
18 buildings housing 2,300 high quality
apartments and Park Hyatt London
River Thames.
This scheme will contribute to the
existing skyline of Vauxhall. The
inclusion of the Linear Park shops,
Offices, and a GP's Surgery will create
a sense of place.

NEXT CHAPTER OF NINE ELMS

TODAY
2021

At 35m above the ground, the 25m-long Sky Pool is a world first. Residents have complained that heating the pool in winter costs £450 per day

Nine Elms Lane

Nine Elms Lane at night: Towers and wide roads contribute to a feeling that the character of the development does not read as London

Featuring the winners of The Pineapples awards for place 2021

The Pineapples celebrate places that thrive, that contribute to urban life and that make a positive social and environmental impact

Supported by

Paul Monaghan, AHMM, accepts the Pineapple for Place of the Year for Television Centre in White City

Tim Wilson from Copeland Park accepts the Pineapple for Creative Reuse for the Copeland Park and Bussey Building in London

Liam Ronan-Chlond, First Base, collects the Pineapple for Community Engagment for Soapworks in Bristol

Jude Barber, Collective Architecture, accepts the Pineapple for Future Place for Granton Waterfront in Edinburgh

The winners of The Pineapples 2021 awards for place, supported by the Design Council, were announced on Friday, 16 July at an online awards ceremony. Shortlisted projects for The Pineapples presented live to the judges and audience as part of the programme of the Festival of Place: The Pineapples, which ran online from 12-16 July, 2021.

The Pineapples celebrate the urban life of developments and places where people want to live, work and play. The nine categories are activation, community engagement, creative reuse, future place, international future place, place in progress, place of the year, public space and sustainable transport.

The Design Council said: "We are proud to sponsor the Festival of Place and the Pineapple Awards. Our experience and evidence shows that well-designed neighbourhoods can have a transformational impact on us all, improving health and wellbeing, enhancing the environment and stimulating the economy."

Special thanks to our judges
Vicky Brown, MAKE Architects

Minnie Moll, chief executive of the Design Council, hosted the awards alongside editor-in-chief Christine Murray and a pineapple

Aminah Ricks, Future Planners
Blossom Young, Poplar HARCA
Magali Thomson, Great Ormond Street
    Hospital
Catherine Max, Catherine Max Consulting
Hazel Rounding, Shedkm
Maja Naumczyk, Falkirk Council
Pete Swift, Planit-ie
Dan Anderson, Fourth Street
Cannon Ivers, LDA Design
Sophie Thompson, LDA Design
Sarah Jones-Morris, Landsmith Associates
Elizabeth Rapoport, Homes England
Kelly Clark, Sustrans
Justin Nicholls, Fathom Architects
Julian Tollast, Quintain
Jonny McKenna, Metropolitan Workshop
Ben Adams, Ben Adams Architects
Hani Salih, Migrants Bureau
Phil Stallwood, CEG
Kapila Perera, Design Council
Will Sandy, Will Sandy Design Studio
Pamela Smith, National Trust
Martha Thorne, IE University
Christopher Arthey, Axiom Developments
Dominic Spray, Hadley Property Group
Daisy Narayanan, City of Edinburgh

The Pineapple for Place of the Year

Television Centre, White City– Stanhope, Mitsui Fudosan, AIMCo, BBC Studioworks
with Allford Hall Monaghan Morris
Television Centre has opened to the public while continuing to be a place of work, with
the BBC still making programmes within the refurbished studios. The development's
external spaces have become the backdrop for some of the nation's most-watched and
loved television shows, including *Strictly Come Dancing* and *Top Gear*. Shows are now
undertaken in the open-air, overlooked by residential apartments and watched by the
general public.

Judges' comments: "A truly
rounded delivery of
reinvention of perception,
retained iconic identity
and creation of vibrancy
whilst also setting up wider
demographic connections"

West Green Place, Haringey –
Pocket Living with HTA Design
The regeneration of what was council-owned
brownfield land into a residential street that
provides community uses and connects to
Downhills Park.

Ram Quarter, Wandsworth –
Greenland UK with EPR Architects
The former Young's brewery site has been
transformed into a residential quarter that
celebrates its heritage while creating a vibrant
new heart in Wandsworth town centre.

MediaCity UK, Salford –
Peel Media: Peel L&P and Legal & General
Capital
In the decade since the first TV show was
broadcast from MediaCityUK it has evolved
into a vibrant community where people live,
work, study and spend their leisure time.

The Pineapple for Place in Progress

Winner: Climate Innovation District, Leeds – Citu Group Developments
This district consists of family homes, apartments, The Place - a large zero carbon office building and centre for excellence in tackling climate change, retail spaces, a primary school, a care home and a community centre. It spans both banks of the River Aire and is designed to reduce carbon emissions at every stage.

Judges' comments:
"The Climate Innovation District is setting the pace for sustainable and healthy development, and proving that sustainability can, and should, be beautiful. We applaud Citu for changing the way communities live while providing a low carbon and attractive environment"

Place in Progress finalists

Barking Riverside, London – Barking
Riverside
Expected to be completed within 15 years,
this 180-hectare mixed-use development sits
alongside 2km of Thames River frontage in
east London, with 10,000 homes planned.

Circus Street, Brighton – U+I with shedkm
This mixed-use development is transforming
a derelict area of Brighton into a bespoke new
quarter. It aims to maximise the public space
embedding the value of community and social
interaction at the heart of the scheme.

New Islington, Manchester – House by
Urban Splash
This mixed-use project has transformed
a once deprived area to one of the UK's
most desirable and accessible mixed-tenure
communities.

The Old Vinyl Factory, London – U+I
This mixed-use neighbourhood with over 700
homes, 50,000m² of offices, an innovation
hub, an academy school, along with shops,
cafes and a health centre, has transformed a
derelict 7-hectare ex-EMI factory site.

**Sighthill Transformation Regeneration
Masterplan**, Glasgow – Glasgow City Council
and Keepmoat Homes Scotland with LDA
Design
This landscape-led masterplan transforms
Sighthill, with a mix of 850 new homes,
education and community facilities, along
with extensive parklands.

The Pineapple for Future Place

Winner: Granton Waterfront, Edinburgh – City of Edinburgh Council with Collective Architecture
The proposal for Granton Waterfront includes 3,000 new homes, a new school, cultural facilities and a new
10-hectare flood-resilient coastal park that reconnects the waterfront with the city and existing communities.

Judges' comments:
"A hugely ambitious project that takes a genuine and comprehensive approach to inclusion and social equity, from its considered approach to education and lifelong learning, to the way it gives surrounding communities free access to the sea"

Winner: Love Wolverton, Wolverton – TOWN
The Agora Centre, a 1970s shopping and leisure centre, will be replaced by a grid of residential streets with 115 homes, eight new shop units and a community space. A community energy services company, Wolverton Community Energy, will run the on-site microgrid.

Judges' comments:
"The quality of the design shows honesty and respect for its surroundings with a quality of design that reflects the heritage of the place without pastiche"

Future Place finalists

Better Queensway, Southend-on-Sea –
Porters Place LLP: joint venture between
Swan Housing and Southend-on-Sea
Borough Council
A 1960s council estate will see four tower
blocks demolished and the construction of
1,760 homes, 10,000m² of commercial space,
children's play areas, parks and public spaces.

Blackwell Yard, Poplar –
Hadley Property Group
Plans for this 1.9-hectare site include a new
river boat pier, a community hub and primary
school, homes and workspace and a wellness
centre, transforming this riverside site on the
north bank of the river Thames, which was a
private car park for more than 30 years.

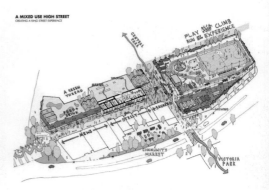

High Path Estate, Merton –
Clarion Housing Group with PRP Architects
This development seeks to keep the existing
community in situ and rehouse them first.
The masterplan will reconnect existing
neighbourhoods with a series of new streets
and create a new park.

Station Hill, Reading –
Lincoln MGT with CallisonRTKL
Located just steps from Reading's mainline
train station, Station Hill includes offices,
retail spaces, 750 homes and 0.8 hectares
of public realm. The project is on track for a
BREEAM Excellent rating.

Stretford Masterplan –
Bruntwood Works and Trafford Council JV
This masterplan aims to transform Stretford
Mall into a high street to create a self-sufficient
and sustainable town centre with revitalised
retail, solar street lighting, district heating
systems, 800 homes and public spaces.

International Future Place finalists

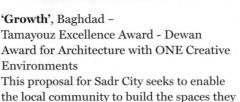

'Growth', Baghdad –
Tamayouz Excellence Award - Dewan
Award for Architecture with ONE Creative
Environments
This proposal for Sadr City seeks to enable
the local community to build the spaces they
require using vernacular materials.

The Depot, Bucharest –
KAP Studios
This city-scale, £500 million project will
transform disused railway lands and old
warehouses into a new neighbourhood with
a mix of homes, shopping, offices, a music
venue, hotels, healthcare and education.

The Pineapple for International Future Place

Winner: Lyon Confluence, Lyon – Bouygues Immobilier, Linkcity with David Chipperfield Architects
This mixed-use quarter contains a range of housing tenures, offices and a health centre, and within each block, the buildings are grouped to define garden courtyards. Transparent and permeable ground-floors give access to the gardens from the street and help to animate the surrounding public spaces.

Judges' comments: "There is a good mix of uses, from social housing to offices and a health centre, and a diversity of landscaped spaces, from formal plazas to informal places to private gardens, with a nice flow that should connect up from a nature and biodiversity perspective"

The Pineapple for Activation

Winner: Centre of Gravity, Soapworks, Bristol – First Base
A month-long exhibition in the Soapworks building with local art collective Centre of Gravity provided a
showcase for 60 artists and was curated as a mix of inspiring contemporary art, film talks and performance.

Judges' comments:
"The project has an impact
beyond its location and has
helped to build confidence
and skills among the local
artists and community,
and although the exhibition
was only a month long, its
impact should be felt for
much longer"

Activation finalists

Box on the Docks, Salford – Peel Media
In June 2020, within two months of the idea
being conceived, MediaCityUK delivered 30
sheds and greenhouses transformed by local
artists as dining pods for their restaurants
as well as an immersive children's art trail to
rebuild visitor confidence and drive footfall.

Sayer Street & Meadow, London –
Lendlease with Michael Grubb Studio
The Meadow is a playable landscape that
links to Sayer Street, a contemporary
reinterpretation of a modern high street.
The result is a playful linear folly offering
creative places to meet, work and browse.

Beckenham Place Mansion, London –
Copeland
This Grade II* listed Georgian building has
been reinvented as an artistic and community
hub including eight resident solo artists,
a sewing school and a multi-use space for
yoga, dance, youth theatre and more.

Mayfield, Manchester – The Mayfield
Partnership
A historic depot building has been reimagined
as a cultural destination with a food market,
bars, cultural spaces and more, including the
depot itself which provides a covered space for
700 visitors.

The Bird Box, Bromsgrove – Bromsgrove
District Council and North Worcestershire
Economic Development and Regeneration
(NWeDR) with ONE Creative Environments
The Bird Box adds creative seating, a stage
and open areas, transforming an unattractive
site in Bromsgrove town centre.

The Pineapple for Sustainable Transport

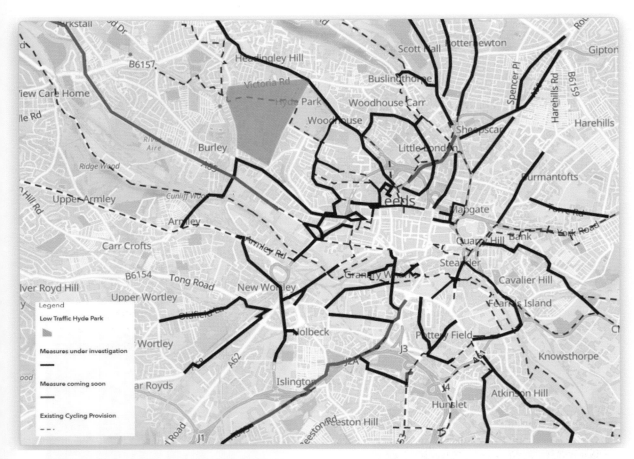

Legend

Low Traffic Hyde Park

Measures under investigation

Measure coming soon

Existing Cycling Provision

Winner: Connecting Leeds COVID Response, Leeds – Leeds City Council with Commonplace
The greatest success of this project has been the ability to adapt, change, and respond to the dynamic needs of the community during a time of immense national and international uncertainty. Connecting Leeds is ambitious, a long-term transport strategy, but with an ability to scale and adapt that makes it dynamic and responsive to change.

Judges' comments:
"The project is going about this transformation in the right ways, implementing test projects and through extensive community consultation. The scale and holistic approach to encouraging a shift to active travel coupled with investment in significant infrastructure made this an exciting project"

Sustainable Transport finalists

CYCLE42 , London – Hadley Property Group
Launched during the pandemic, CYCLE42 is the result of cross-sector collaboration between Hadley Property Group, Clarion Housing Group, Brompton Bike Hire and multiple charities, who came together to offer free bikes for hire to Merton residents.

West Gorton Community Park, Manchester – Manchester City Council with BDP
This park pedestrianises roads and improves sightlines to encourage cycling and walking. It's also the first UK demonstrator project for the GrowGreen initiative, which will evaluate stormwater flows, air quality, biodiversity and contributes to community value.

The Northbank Low Emission Neighbourhood, London –
The Northbank BID
The Northbank BID worked with both GLA and Westminster City Council to tackle local pollution and exposure to pollution, developing a Business Low Emission Neighbourhood (BLEN).

The Pineapple for Community Engagement

Winner: Soapworks, Bristol – First Base
Soapworks used the bespoke app Give-My-View, an engagement tool developed by First Base with Built-ID, alongside consultation meetings, newsletters, phone calls and posted information resulting in almost 6,000 responses to proposals.

Judges' comments: "An impressive and thoughtful approach which pays careful attention to the needs of the community - from affordable housing, flexible small-scale retail offerings and increased public space options for our Covid reality. It's an expansive yet sensitive project"

Community Engagement finalists

Active Streets , Edinburgh – Parsons Green
Parent Council with New Practice, Sustrans,
Transport for Scotland and City of Edinburgh
Council
Local community members had their say on
making sustainable everyday journeys.

**Shaping the Heart of Nottingham
Waterside**, Trent Basin, Nottingham –
Blueprint with Deetu
Feedback from local communities via
digital engagement on the redevelopment of
Nottingham's waterside.

The Nicholson Quarter, Maidenhead –
Areli Real Estate with JTP
Community planning weekends and
workshops have been informing the vision
to transform a 1960s shopping centre into a
mixed-use masterplan.

BlockWest, Bristol – Making Together with
Knowle West residents, We Can Make and
Automated Architecture
A digital design and modular construction kit
enabled locals to design and build a Covid-
safe community pavilion.

The Bermondsey Project, London –
Grosvenor Britain & Ireland
Seven years of community engagement
is now feeding into the creation of a
community forum to guide phase one of the
regeneration project.

The Pineapple for Creative Reuse

Winner: Copeland Park & Bussey Building, Peckham – Copeland Park
This reuse project offers a wide variety of mixed-use spaces for creative and cultural events
including a gallery, a warehouse and rooftops. Acting as Peckham's cultural quarter, it
provides countless events, and is a hub for a supportive network of creatives.

Judges' comments:
"The mix of uses and its
vibrancy, as well as the
ambition to keep rents
affordable is admirable.
Amazing to have a
family business running
this space"

Creative Reuse finalists

Hatworks Creative Workspace, Luton –
The Culture Trust
A building that was once an unwelcome
reminder of industrial decline, having last
been occupied in 2006 as a Hat Factory, has
been transformed it into a cultural hotspot for
young entrepreneurs to showcase their work.

Brixton Windmill, London –
Lambeth Council with Squire & Partners
The scheme works to preserve the heritage of
this 200-year-old structure, the last working
windmill in London, while ensuring use by
future generations in providing flexible space
to be used by the wider community.

Roof East, London – Urban Space
Management/London Borough of Newham
This multistorey car park in the middle of
Stratford Centre is now a thriving park and
cultural hotspot with an open-air cinema,
street food and a bar.

The Old Vinyl Factory, London – U+I
This derelict 7-hectare ex-EMI factory site
has become a cultural hub featuring over 700
homes, 50,000m² of offices, an innovation
hub, an academy school, along with shops,
cafes and a health centre

The Pineapple for Public Space

Winner: Cheney Row Park, Waltham Forest – London Borough of Waltham Forest with We Made That
This public space has transformed a former landfill site into a new space with a woodland area, 467 new trees planted in the park, a BMX track and a bespoke and proprietary play kit used by children of all ages. This reinvention of the space has added to the play and enjoyment of the community.

Judges' comments: "The environmentally sensitive design and the creative incorporation of site remediation works to create a playable landscape was really amazing. The environmental and social agendas can sometimes be at odds, but this project brought them together"

Winner: West Gorton Community Park, Manchester – Manchester City Council with BDP
The judges were impressed with this park's social and environmental contribution to the wider place
through the incorporation of biodiversity, SUDS and flood remediation works. They loved the fact that
data was being collected for research that will be shared.

Judges' comments:
"Creating a lovely place
is one thing, but learning
lessons to improve other
public spaces really stands
out. It also makes SUDS
fun. The social and the
environmental go hand-
in-hand which is essential
in tackling the climate
emergency"

Public Space finalists

Higham Hill Theatre, London –
Create and London Borough of Waltham
Forest with vPPR Architects
A neglected plot of land has been transformed
into a community amphitheatre surrounded
by greenery at the edge of a playground,
adding life to the wider community.

Ambrose Walk Community Garden,
London – Malmesbury Residents Association
and Tower Hamlets Homes with Wilder
Communities
This community garden in east London has
been reinvented from being a derelict mass of
tarmac in the centre of social housing.

Christchurch Gardens, London –
City of Westminster and Victoria BID with
ReardonSmith Landscape
This green space, a former burial ground near
Westminster Abbey, reopened to the public in
September 2020 providing a welcoming space
for people to explore, enjoy and learn.

Chelsea Barracks, London –
Qatari Diar Development Company with
Squire & Partners
The gardens form an integral part of this
5-hectare masterplan, aiming to improve the
environment for locals, businesses and the
wider community.

Membership is designed for organisations that want to invest in learning, gain fresh thinking and join a wider community of purpose-driven professionals striving to make a positive impact on places.

As a member, you'll gain free access to all Festival of Place events, including passes to all digital and in-person events, plus digital access to our amazing video talks library.

And a host of other benefits across The Developer.

FESTIVAL OF PLACE

Become a member

Annual membership includes access to:
Festival of place: Social Impact, 1-3 Mar, 2022
Festival of place, 6 July, 2022, London
Festival of place: Climate Resilience, Nov, 2022
Festival of place: member only events

Invest in your people, meet likeminded collaborators and learn.

Full membership package can be found at:
www.festivalofplace.co.uk
Or contact james@thedeveloper.live

Powered by:

the developer

In the photobooth:
Hackney Bridge

Marco Ferrari talks to workers
and passers-by as they visit the
photobooth at Hackney Bridge,
a canal-side workspace, food
and shopping destination in the
Queen Elizabeth Olympic Park

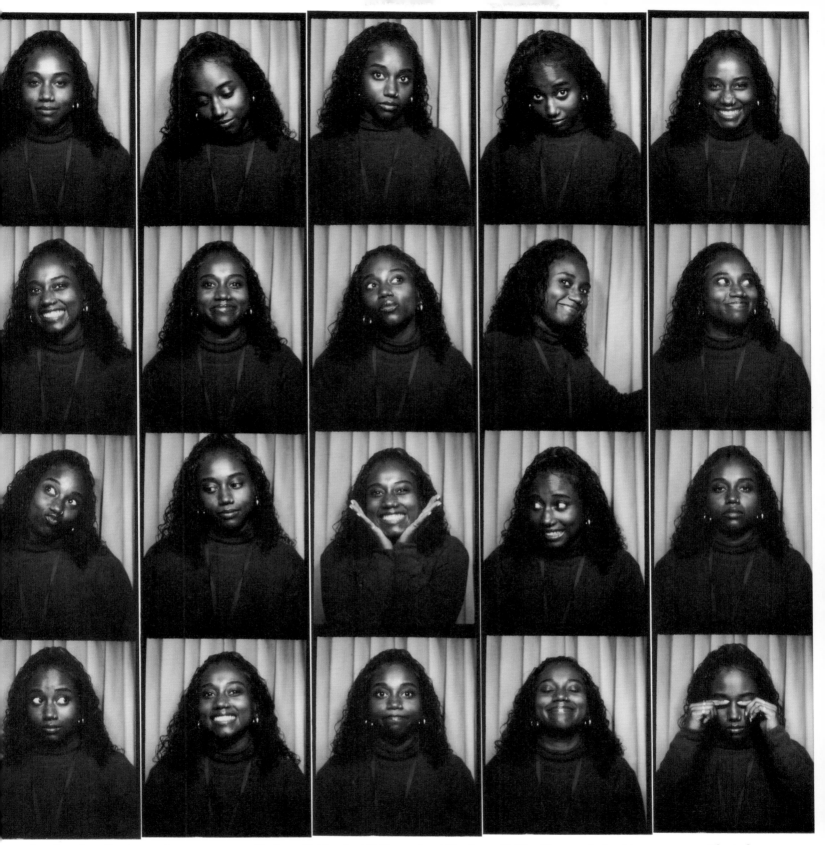

In the photobooth Rianna, duty manager at Hackney Bridge (23) **Tell me about Hackney Bridge** It opened about two years ago. The indoor food and beverage area has been open for five months. It's growing quickly for a space that's so new. We have our co-working space, we have our charities, our office building, retail space and also food and beverage. There is a lot of interest and people are always asking how they can get involved so I think it's going really well **What do you like best about your job?** Watching the place grow and being a part of it, having ideas and working with people to make them happen **What's the future of Hackney Bridge?** There's the renovation of the garden space on the canal. We're going to have a basketball court and a nice seating area for people to enjoy themselves in the beer garden **Why should people come to Hackney Bridge?** People should come because it has a lot to offer and it's very community focused, everyone is included all the time. There is something for everyone, so you will never feel left out

In the photobooth Lauren, a doctor (31), Tom (30) and Smidge, a Pembroke Welsh corgi **Where are you from?** Tom: I was born in France and I've been in London for six years. Lauren: I'm originally from Enfield **What brought you here today?** Tom: We live in West Ham which is 20 minutes walk away. We were walking our dog around here. Lauren: We both rented around here before we bought **Did you know about Hackney Bridge?** Tom: We didn't realise what it was. Then some friends told us about this photobooth and we wanted to come and take pictures. There's a lot more going on than we thought. Just got my hair cut **Is there anything you would change about the area?** Tom: It's changed a lot since the Olympics, and I think the way it's gone is beneficial for a lot of people. Unfortunately it out-prices a lot of people who used to live around here, but the rejuvenation and the amount of young people it brings, businesses and all that, I think it's made a really positive impact. Lauren: They are building more taller flats that could potentially ruin the atmosphere a bit. It's quite a hipster area, it has a quite nice feel to it **Do you feel there is a sense of community in this part of London?** Lauren: Yes, definitely. Tom: I think there is, especially since we got the dog. We go to East Village and a lot of people meet up there with their dogs. There are Instagram groups and WhatsApp groups and everyone is really friendly and trying to make the most out of it and have an enjoyable kind of life

In the photobooth Indya (24) and Leela (21) **What brought you here today?** Leela: I live in Kent with our parents and we all came to visit Indya. Indya: I live close by, they came for lunch and now we're just out for a walk with the dog **Have you been here before?** Indya: Not to Hackney Bridge specifically, we've been to Hackney Wick and around the canal. But I knew there was a photobooth here and we wanted to take photos of all of us together **What's your feeling about this area?** Indya: I haven't lived here for that long but it does feel safe, there is a community kind of feel, so I can say that I'm happy that I moved around here

In the photobooth Umberto (42), owner of the Wicked Bike Repair shop at Hackney Bridge @wicked_bike_repair **Where are you from?** I'm originally from Italy, I used to live right here, but I just moved across Hackney Marshes towards Walthamstow **Can you tell me more about Wicked Bike Repair?** This is my first shop, however the company is older than the shop. I started this company working from home and then built up enough customers and saved enough money to open a proper shop **Why Hackney Bridge?** First of all, because I live in the area. One of my customers suggested I apply for a space here. I was also interested in the project as a community-oriented space. I thought it could be a great platform not only for me but for the neighbourhood. There is a community spirit especially between the members. We all know each other and we all help each other whenever we can **How does the future of Hackney Bridge look for you?** There is still a lot of potential, we have not peaked yet and I feel it's going to grow a lot in the next year. The future looks exciting. I love this place